Free Gift!

Want a free gift?

Email us at
betterlifejournals@gmail.com

Title the email "Journal" and we will send you
something fun!

Visit our website for more:
https://lifelabmagazine.com/better-life-
journals/

More Journals!

Want a Journal to give your busy friend or family member as a gift, or just want more Journal ideas?

Check out some of our other Journals...

90 Day Better Career Journal
90 Day Daily Positivity Journal
90 Day Self Discovery Journal
90 Day Healthy Habit Journal
90 Day Mental Health Journal
Your 90 Day Daily Victory Journal
Your 365 Day Wellbeing Journal

Choose from different lengths (60 days, 90 days and yearly) as well as different types of journals (with different goals and objectives). You are sure to find something that'll be great both as a personal journal and as a gift!

YOUR WEEKLY WORK-LIFE BALANCE CHECKLIST

Nobody really cares if you're miserable, so you might as well be happy

CYNTHIA NELMS

GETTING STARTED

The workbook and journal is pretty self-explanatory so you can just go through it at your own pace. That said, here are some tips that can help you get the most out of this:

- **Schedule a specific time** in the day when you will work on this workbook over the coming days. Having a specific time will help you stay on course. An easy way to do this is to schedule a recurring reminder on your phone's calendar.
- Start with the **Personal Assessment**.
- Next, work on the empowering **habit creator** section. This can help you create one good habit over the next 90 days, which will have a big impact on your wellbeing and happiness.
- Go through the Wellbeing activities list to get ideas for what you can do to take better care of yourself.
- Complete the journal pages every week (ideally daily) over the coming days. Take a bit of time before you get started to mentally prepare yourself if you need to but once you start, commit to doing them every day.

Most importantly, take it one day at a time. Small actions overtime will get you big results, as you will soon find out :)

Let's begin!

DREAM BIG,
WORK HARD,
MAKE IT
happen.

PERSONAL ASSESSMENT

1. What does work-life balance mean to me?

2. What does having more balance look like?

3. Current level of balance   1 2 3 4 5

4. Desired level of balance   1 2 3 4 5

PERSONAL ASSESSMENT

5. Why is it important for me to have more work-life balance?

6. Who is the most balanced person I know, and what do I like most about them/their life?

7. What are the things I can do regularly to be more balanced (both both big and small, like completing the journal every day)?

DECLARATION

I hereby commit to this daily practice to have more work-life balance.

Sign:

Date:

DO
YOUR BEST

☆ EMPOWERING ☆ HABIT CREATOR

Pick one small thing you can do every day for the next 90 days, something that will make you feel good (e.g. gratitude log, meditation, random acts of kindness, etc).

Once you have decided, use the habit tracker below to stick to this small daily positive habit by ticking/coloring one box for every day you practice the habit.

ONE THING = ________________________________

1

30

60

90

enjoy every moment.

WELLBEING ACTIVITIES

Make a list of things that make you feel happy/good (we've included some ideas to get you started).

This list will come in very handy when planning your daily activities, and especially on days you aren't feeling so good (we all have off days, so it's ok).

- ○ Workout (even a 3-5 minutes of physical exercise can have a positive impact on your mood, and wellbeing)

- ○ Practice gratitude (practicing gratitude can not only help you feel good in the short term, but in the long term too!)

- ○ Meditation (practicing meditation can help you to regulate your emotions, and stress, better)

- ○ Random acts of kindness (being nice & helping others is one of the best ways, if not the best way, to feel joy)

- ○ Enjoy a nice cup of your favorite tea or coffee (even small things like this can have a big impact on your mood)

- ○

- ○

WELLBEING ACTIVITIES

Let your
light
Shine

START YOUR JOURNEY!

WEEK OF:

MY PRIORITIES FOR THIS WEEK

GRATITUDE LOG:

MAIN GOALS:

DAILY ACTIVITIES

	M	T	W	T	F	S	S
Daily gratitude log	○	○	○	○	○	○	○
Do something fun	○	○	○	○	○	○	○
8 glasses of water	○	○	○	○	○	○	○
Meditate	○	○	○	○	○	○	○
Daily journaling	○	○	○	○	○	○	○
Exercise	○	○	○	○	○	○	○
Do something important	○	○	○	○	○	○	○
Do something good	○	○	○	○	○	○	○
Eat healthy	○	○	○	○	○	○	○
Read/listen to something good	○	○	○	○	○	○	○
Connect with others	○	○	○	○	○	○	○

MY PRIORITIES FOR THIS WEEK

GRATITUDE LOG:

MAIN GOALS:

DAILY ACTIVITIES

	M	T	W	T	F	S	S
Daily gratitude log	○	○	○	○	○	○	○
Do something fun	○	○	○	○	○	○	○
8 glasses of water	○	○	○	○	○	○	○
Meditate	○	○	○	○	○	○	○
Daily journaling	○	○	○	○	○	○	○
Exercise	○	○	○	○	○	○	○
Do something important	○	○	○	○	○	○	○
Do something good	○	○	○	○	○	○	○
Eat healthy	○	○	○	○	○	○	○
Read/listen to something good	○	○	○	○	○	○	○
Connect with others	○	○	○	○	○	○	○

MY PRIORITIES FOR THIS WEEK

GRATITUDE LOG:

MAIN GOALS:

DAILY ACTIVITIES

	M	T	W	T	F	S	S
Daily gratitude log	○	○	○	○	○	○	○
Do something fun	○	○	○	○	○	○	○
8 glasses of water	○	○	○	○	○	○	○
Meditate	○	○	○	○	○	○	○
Daily journaling	○	○	○	○	○	○	○
Exercise	○	○	○	○	○	○	○
Do something important	○	○	○	○	○	○	○
Do something good	○	○	○	○	○	○	○
Eat healthy	○	○	○	○	○	○	○
Read/listen to something good	○	○	○	○	○	○	○
Connect with others	○	○	○	○	○	○	○

MY PRIORITIES FOR THIS WEEK

GRATITUDE LOG:

MAIN GOALS:

DAILY ACTIVITIES

	M	T	W	T	F	S	S
Daily gratitude log	○	○	○	○	○	○	○
Do something fun	○	○	○	○	○	○	○
8 glasses of water	○	○	○	○	○	○	○
Meditate	○	○	○	○	○	○	○
Daily journaling	○	○	○	○	○	○	○
Exercise	○	○	○	○	○	○	○
Do something important	○	○	○	○	○	○	○
Do something good	○	○	○	○	○	○	○
Eat healthy	○	○	○	○	○	○	○
Read/listen to something good	○	○	○	○	○	○	○
Connect with others	○	○	○	○	○	○	○

WEEK OF:

MY PRIORITIES FOR THIS WEEK

GRATITUDE LOG:

MAIN GOALS:

DAILY ACTIVITIES

	M	T	W	T	F	S	S
Daily gratitude log	○	○	○	○	○	○	○
Do something fun	○	○	○	○	○	○	○
8 glasses of water	○	○	○	○	○	○	○
Meditate	○	○	○	○	○	○	○
Daily journaling	○	○	○	○	○	○	○
Exercise	○	○	○	○	○	○	○
Do something important	○	○	○	○	○	○	○
Do something good	○	○	○	○	○	○	○
Eat healthy	○	○	○	○	○	○	○
Read/listen to something good	○	○	○	○	○	○	○
Connect with others	○	○	○	○	○	○	○

WEEK OF:

MY PRIORITIES FOR THIS WEEK

GRATITUDE LOG:

MAIN GOALS:

DAILY ACTIVITIES

          M T W T F S S

Daily gratitude log
Do something fun
8 glasses of water
Meditate
Daily journaling
Exercise
Do something
important
Do something good
Eat healthy
Read/listen
to something good
Connect with others

WEEK OF:

MY PRIORITIES FOR THIS WEEK

GRATITUDE LOG:

MAIN GOALS:

DAILY ACTIVITIES

	M	T	W	T	F	S	S
Daily gratitude log	○	○	○	○	○	○	○
Do something fun	○	○	○	○	○	○	○
8 glasses of water	○	○	○	○	○	○	○
Meditate	○	○	○	○	○	○	○
Daily journaling	○	○	○	○	○	○	○
Exercise	○	○	○	○	○	○	○
Do something important	○	○	○	○	○	○	○
Do something good	○	○	○	○	○	○	○
Eat healthy	○	○	○	○	○	○	○
Read/listen to something good	○	○	○	○	○	○	○
Connect with others	○	○	○	○	○	○	○

MY PRIORITIES FOR THIS WEEK

GRATITUDE LOG:

MAIN GOALS:

DAILY ACTIVITIES

	M	T	W	T	F	S	S
Daily gratitude log	○	○	○	○	○	○	○
Do something fun	○	○	○	○	○	○	○
8 glasses of water	○	○	○	○	○	○	○
Meditate	○	○	○	○	○	○	○
Daily journaling	○	○	○	○	○	○	○
Exercise	○	○	○	○	○	○	○
Do something important	○	○	○	○	○	○	○
Do something good	○	○	○	○	○	○	○
Eat healthy	○	○	○	○	○	○	○
Read/listen to something good	○	○	○	○	○	○	○
Connect with others	○	○	○	○	○	○	○

MY PRIORITIES FOR THIS WEEK

GRATITUDE LOG:

MAIN GOALS:

DAILY ACTIVITIES

	M	T	W	T	F	S	S
Daily gratitude log	○	○	○	○	○	○	○
Do something fun	○	○	○	○	○	○	○
8 glasses of water	○	○	○	○	○	○	○
Meditate	○	○	○	○	○	○	○
Daily journaling	○	○	○	○	○	○	○
Exercise	○	○	○	○	○	○	○
Do something important	○	○	○	○	○	○	○
Do something good	○	○	○	○	○	○	○
Eat healthy	○	○	○	○	○	○	○
Read/listen to something good	○	○	○	○	○	○	○
Connect with others	○	○	○	○	○	○	○

WEEK OF:

MY PRIORITIES FOR THIS WEEK

GRATITUDE LOG:

MAIN GOALS:

DAILY ACTIVITIES

	M	T	W	T	F	S	S
Daily gratitude log	○	○	○	○	○	○	○
Do something fun	○	○	○	○	○	○	○
8 glasses of water	○	○	○	○	○	○	○
Meditate	○	○	○	○	○	○	○
Daily journaling	○	○	○	○	○	○	○
Exercise	○	○	○	○	○	○	○
Do something important	○	○	○	○	○	○	○
Do something good	○	○	○	○	○	○	○
Eat healthy	○	○	○	○	○	○	○
Read/listen to something good	○	○	○	○	○	○	○
Connect with others	○	○	○	○	○	○	○

WEEK OF:

MY PRIORITIES FOR THIS WEEK

GRATITUDE LOG:

MAIN GOALS:

DAILY ACTIVITIES

	M	T	W	T	F	S	S
Daily gratitude log	○	○	○	○	○	○	○
Do something fun	○	○	○	○	○	○	○
8 glasses of water	○	○	○	○	○	○	○
Meditate	○	○	○	○	○	○	○
Daily journaling	○	○	○	○	○	○	○
Exercise	○	○	○	○	○	○	○
Do something important	○	○	○	○	○	○	○
Do something good	○	○	○	○	○	○	○
Eat healthy	○	○	○	○	○	○	○
Read/listen to something good	○	○	○	○	○	○	○
Connect with others	○	○	○	○	○	○	○

WEEK OF:

MY PRIORITIES FOR THIS WEEK

GRATITUDE LOG:

MAIN GOALS:

DAILY ACTIVITIES

M T W T F S S

Daily gratitude log
Do something fun
8 glasses of water
Meditate
Daily journaling
Exercise
Do something
important
Do something good
Eat healthy
Read/listen
to something good
Connect with others

MY PRIORITIES FOR THIS WEEK

GRATITUDE LOG:

MAIN GOALS:

DAILY ACTIVITIES

	M	T	W	T	F	S	S
Daily gratitude log	○	○	○	○	○	○	○
Do something fun	○	○	○	○	○	○	○
8 glasses of water	○	○	○	○	○	○	○
Meditate	○	○	○	○	○	○	○
Daily journaling	○	○	○	○	○	○	○
Exercise	○	○	○	○	○	○	○
Do something important	○	○	○	○	○	○	○
Do something good	○	○	○	○	○	○	○
Eat healthy	○	○	○	○	○	○	○
Read/listen to something good	○	○	○	○	○	○	○
Connect with others	○	○	○	○	○	○	○

MY PRIORITIES FOR THIS WEEK

GRATITUDE LOG:

MAIN GOALS:

DAILY ACTIVITIES

	M	T	W	T	F	S	S
Daily gratitude log	○	○	○	○	○	○	○
Do something fun	○	○	○	○	○	○	○
8 glasses of water	○	○	○	○	○	○	○
Meditate	○	○	○	○	○	○	○
Daily journaling	○	○	○	○	○	○	○
Exercise	○	○	○	○	○	○	○
Do something important	○	○	○	○	○	○	○
Do something good	○	○	○	○	○	○	○
Eat healthy	○	○	○	○	○	○	○
Read/listen to something good	○	○	○	○	○	○	○
Connect with others	○	○	○	○	○	○	○

WEEK OF:

MY PRIORITIES FOR THIS WEEK

GRATITUDE LOG:

MAIN GOALS:

DAILY ACTIVITIES

	M	T	W	T	F	S	S
Daily gratitude log	○	○	○	○	○	○	○
Do something fun	○	○	○	○	○	○	○
8 glasses of water	○	○	○	○	○	○	○
Meditate	○	○	○	○	○	○	○
Daily journaling	○	○	○	○	○	○	○
Exercise	○	○	○	○	○	○	○
Do something important	○	○	○	○	○	○	○
Do something good	○	○	○	○	○	○	○
Eat healthy	○	○	○	○	○	○	○
Read/listen to something good	○	○	○	○	○	○	○
Connect with others	○	○	○	○	○	○	○

WEEK OF:

MY PRIORITIES FOR THIS WEEK

GRATITUDE LOG:

MAIN GOALS:

DAILY ACTIVITIES

M T W T F S S

Daily gratitude log
Do something fun
8 glasses of water
Meditate
Daily journaling
Exercise
Do something important
Do something good
Eat healthy
Read/listen to something good
Connect with others

WEEK OF:

MY PRIORITIES FOR THIS WEEK

GRATITUDE LOG:

MAIN GOALS:

DAILY ACTIVITIES

	M	T	W	T	F	S	S
Daily gratitude log	○	○	○	○	○	○	○
Do something fun	○	○	○	○	○	○	○
8 glasses of water	○	○	○	○	○	○	○
Meditate	○	○	○	○	○	○	○
Daily journaling	○	○	○	○	○	○	○
Exercise	○	○	○	○	○	○	○
Do something important	○	○	○	○	○	○	○
Do something good	○	○	○	○	○	○	○
Eat healthy	○	○	○	○	○	○	○
Read/listen to something good	○	○	○	○	○	○	○
Connect with others	○	○	○	○	○	○	○

WEEK OF:

MY PRIORITIES FOR THIS WEEK

GRATITUDE LOG:

MAIN GOALS:

DAILY ACTIVITIES

M T W T F S S

Daily gratitude log
Do something fun
8 glasses of water
Meditate
Daily journaling
Exercise
Do something important
Do something good
Eat healthy
Read/listen to something good
Connect with others

MY PRIORITIES FOR THIS WEEK

GRATITUDE LOG:

MAIN GOALS:

DAILY ACTIVITIES

	M	T	W	T	F	S	S
Daily gratitude log	○	○	○	○	○	○	○
Do something fun	○	○	○	○	○	○	○
8 glasses of water	○	○	○	○	○	○	○
Meditate	○	○	○	○	○	○	○
Daily journaling	○	○	○	○	○	○	○
Exercise	○	○	○	○	○	○	○
Do something important	○	○	○	○	○	○	○
Do something good	○	○	○	○	○	○	○
Eat healthy	○	○	○	○	○	○	○
Read/listen to something good	○	○	○	○	○	○	○
Connect with others	○	○	○	○	○	○	○

MY PRIORITIES FOR THIS WEEK

GRATITUDE LOG:

MAIN GOALS:

DAILY ACTIVITIES

	M	T	W	T	F	S	S
Daily gratitude log	○	○	○	○	○	○	○
Do something fun	○	○	○	○	○	○	○
8 glasses of water	○	○	○	○	○	○	○
Meditate	○	○	○	○	○	○	○
Daily journaling	○	○	○	○	○	○	○
Exercise	○	○	○	○	○	○	○
Do something important	○	○	○	○	○	○	○
Do something good	○	○	○	○	○	○	○
Eat healthy	○	○	○	○	○	○	○
Read/listen to something good	○	○	○	○	○	○	○
Connect with others	○	○	○	○	○	○	○

WEEK OF:

MY PRIORITIES FOR THIS WEEK

GRATITUDE LOG:

MAIN GOALS:

DAILY ACTIVITIES

M T W T F S S

Daily gratitude log
Do something fun
8 glasses of water
Meditate
Daily journaling
Exercise
Do something
important
Do something good
Eat healthy
Read/listen
to something good
Connect with others

WEEK OF:

MY PRIORITIES FOR THIS WEEK

GRATITUDE LOG:

MAIN GOALS:

DAILY ACTIVITIES

	M	T	W	T	F	S	S
Daily gratitude log	○	○	○	○	○	○	○
Do something fun	○	○	○	○	○	○	○
8 glasses of water	○	○	○	○	○	○	○
Meditate	○	○	○	○	○	○	○
Daily journaling	○	○	○	○	○	○	○
Exercise	○	○	○	○	○	○	○
Do something important	○	○	○	○	○	○	○
Do something good	○	○	○	○	○	○	○
Eat healthy	○	○	○	○	○	○	○
Read/listen to something good	○	○	○	○	○	○	○
Connect with others	○	○	○	○	○	○	○

MY PRIORITIES FOR THIS WEEK

GRATITUDE LOG:

MAIN GOALS:

DAILY ACTIVITIES

	M	T	W	T	F	S	S
Daily gratitude log	○	○	○	○	○	○	○
Do something fun	○	○	○	○	○	○	○
8 glasses of water	○	○	○	○	○	○	○
Meditate	○	○	○	○	○	○	○
Daily journaling	○	○	○	○	○	○	○
Exercise	○	○	○	○	○	○	○
Do something important	○	○	○	○	○	○	○
Do something good	○	○	○	○	○	○	○
Eat healthy	○	○	○	○	○	○	○
Read/listen to something good	○	○	○	○	○	○	○
Connect with others	○	○	○	○	○	○	○

MY PRIORITIES FOR THIS WEEK

GRATITUDE LOG:

MAIN GOALS:

DAILY ACTIVITIES

	M	T	W	T	F	S	S
Daily gratitude log	○	○	○	○	○	○	○
Do something fun	○	○	○	○	○	○	○
8 glasses of water	○	○	○	○	○	○	○
Meditate	○	○	○	○	○	○	○
Daily journaling	○	○	○	○	○	○	○
Exercise	○	○	○	○	○	○	○
Do something important	○	○	○	○	○	○	○
Do something good	○	○	○	○	○	○	○
Eat healthy	○	○	○	○	○	○	○
Read/listen to something good	○	○	○	○	○	○	○
Connect with others	○	○	○	○	○	○	○

WEEK OF:

MY PRIORITIES FOR THIS WEEK

GRATITUDE LOG:

MAIN GOALS:

DAILY ACTIVITIES

	M	T	W	T	F	S	S
Daily gratitude log	○	○	○	○	○	○	○
Do something fun	○	○	○	○	○	○	○
8 glasses of water	○	○	○	○	○	○	○
Meditate	○	○	○	○	○	○	○
Daily journaling	○	○	○	○	○	○	○
Exercise	○	○	○	○	○	○	○
Do something important	○	○	○	○	○	○	○
Do something good	○	○	○	○	○	○	○
Eat healthy	○	○	○	○	○	○	○
Read/listen to something good	○	○	○	○	○	○	○
Connect with others	○	○	○	○	○	○	○

WEEK OF:

MY PRIORITIES FOR THIS WEEK

GRATITUDE LOG:

MAIN GOALS:

DAILY ACTIVITIES

	M	T	W	T	F	S	S
Daily gratitude log	○	○	○	○	○	○	○
Do something fun	○	○	○	○	○	○	○
8 glasses of water	○	○	○	○	○	○	○
Meditate	○	○	○	○	○	○	○
Daily journaling	○	○	○	○	○	○	○
Exercise	○	○	○	○	○	○	○
Do something important	○	○	○	○	○	○	○
Do something good	○	○	○	○	○	○	○
Eat healthy	○	○	○	○	○	○	○
Read/listen to something good	○	○	○	○	○	○	○
Connect with others	○	○	○	○	○	○	○

WEEK OF:

MY PRIORITIES FOR THIS WEEK

GRATITUDE LOG:

MAIN GOALS:

DAILY ACTIVITIES

	M	T	W	T	F	S	S
Daily gratitude log	○	○	○	○	○	○	○
Do something fun	○	○	○	○	○	○	○
8 glasses of water	○	○	○	○	○	○	○
Meditate	○	○	○	○	○	○	○
Daily journaling	○	○	○	○	○	○	○
Exercise	○	○	○	○	○	○	○
Do something important	○	○	○	○	○	○	○
Do something good	○	○	○	○	○	○	○
Eat healthy	○	○	○	○	○	○	○
Read/listen to something good	○	○	○	○	○	○	○
Connect with others	○	○	○	○	○	○	○

WEEK OF:

MY PRIORITIES FOR THIS WEEK

GRATITUDE LOG:

MAIN GOALS:

DAILY ACTIVITIES

	M	T	W	T	F	S	S
Daily gratitude log	○	○	○	○	○	○	○
Do something fun	○	○	○	○	○	○	○
8 glasses of water	○	○	○	○	○	○	○
Meditate	○	○	○	○	○	○	○
Daily journaling	○	○	○	○	○	○	○
Exercise	○	○	○	○	○	○	○
Do something important	○	○	○	○	○	○	○
Do something good	○	○	○	○	○	○	○
Eat healthy	○	○	○	○	○	○	○
Read/listen to something good	○	○	○	○	○	○	○
Connect with others	○	○	○	○	○	○	○

MY PRIORITIES FOR THIS WEEK

GRATITUDE LOG:

MAIN GOALS:

DAILY ACTIVITIES

	M	T	W	T	F	S	S
Daily gratitude log	○	○	○	○	○	○	○
Do something fun	○	○	○	○	○	○	○
8 glasses of water	○	○	○	○	○	○	○
Meditate	○	○	○	○	○	○	○
Daily journaling	○	○	○	○	○	○	○
Exercise	○	○	○	○	○	○	○
Do something important	○	○	○	○	○	○	○
Do something good	○	○	○	○	○	○	○
Eat healthy	○	○	○	○	○	○	○
Read/listen to something good	○	○	○	○	○	○	○
Connect with others	○	○	○	○	○	○	○

WEEK OF:

MY PRIORITIES FOR THIS WEEK

GRATITUDE LOG:

MAIN GOALS:

DAILY ACTIVITIES

	M	T	W	T	F	S	S
Daily gratitude log	○	○	○	○	○	○	○
Do something fun	○	○	○	○	○	○	○
8 glasses of water	○	○	○	○	○	○	○
Meditate	○	○	○	○	○	○	○
Daily journaling	○	○	○	○	○	○	○
Exercise	○	○	○	○	○	○	○
Do something important	○	○	○	○	○	○	○
Do something good	○	○	○	○	○	○	○
Eat healthy	○	○	○	○	○	○	○
Read/listen to something good	○	○	○	○	○	○	○
Connect with others	○	○	○	○	○	○	○

WEEK OF:

MY PRIORITIES FOR THIS WEEK

GRATITUDE LOG:

MAIN GOALS:

DAILY ACTIVITIES

	M	T	W	T	F	S	S
Daily gratitude log	○	○	○	○	○	○	○
Do something fun	○	○	○	○	○	○	○
8 glasses of water	○	○	○	○	○	○	○
Meditate	○	○	○	○	○	○	○
Daily journaling	○	○	○	○	○	○	○
Exercise	○	○	○	○	○	○	○
Do something important	○	○	○	○	○	○	○
Do something good	○	○	○	○	○	○	○
Eat healthy	○	○	○	○	○	○	○
Read/listen to something good	○	○	○	○	○	○	○
Connect with others	○	○	○	○	○	○	○

WEEK OF:

MY PRIORITIES FOR THIS WEEK

GRATITUDE LOG:

MAIN GOALS:

DAILY ACTIVITIES

	M	T	W	T	F	S	S
Daily gratitude log	○	○	○	○	○	○	○
Do something fun	○	○	○	○	○	○	○
8 glasses of water	○	○	○	○	○	○	○
Meditate	○	○	○	○	○	○	○
Daily journaling	○	○	○	○	○	○	○
Exercise	○	○	○	○	○	○	○
Do something important	○	○	○	○	○	○	○
Do something good	○	○	○	○	○	○	○
Eat healthy	○	○	○	○	○	○	○
Read/listen to something good	○	○	○	○	○	○	○
Connect with others	○	○	○	○	○	○	○

WEEK OF:

MY PRIORITIES FOR THIS WEEK

GRATITUDE LOG:

MAIN GOALS:

DAILY ACTIVITIES

	M	T	W	T	F	S	S
Daily gratitude log	○	○	○	○	○	○	○
Do something fun	○	○	○	○	○	○	○
8 glasses of water	○	○	○	○	○	○	○
Meditate	○	○	○	○	○	○	○
Daily journaling	○	○	○	○	○	○	○
Exercise	○	○	○	○	○	○	○
Do something important	○	○	○	○	○	○	○
Do something good	○	○	○	○	○	○	○
Eat healthy	○	○	○	○	○	○	○
Read/listen to something good	○	○	○	○	○	○	○
Connect with others	○	○	○	○	○	○	○

WEEK OF:

MY PRIORITIES FOR THIS WEEK

GRATITUDE LOG:

MAIN GOALS:

DAILY ACTIVITIES

	M	T	W	T	F	S	S
Daily gratitude log	○	○	○	○	○	○	○
Do something fun	○	○	○	○	○	○	○
8 glasses of water	○	○	○	○	○	○	○
Meditate	○	○	○	○	○	○	○
Daily journaling	○	○	○	○	○	○	○
Exercise	○	○	○	○	○	○	○
Do something important	○	○	○	○	○	○	○
Do something good	○	○	○	○	○	○	○
Eat healthy	○	○	○	○	○	○	○
Read/listen to something good	○	○	○	○	○	○	○
Connect with others	○	○	○	○	○	○	○

WEEK OF:

MY PRIORITIES FOR THIS WEEK

GRATITUDE LOG:

MAIN GOALS:

DAILY ACTIVITIES

	M	T	W	T	F	S	S
Daily gratitude log	○	○	○	○	○	○	○
Do something fun	○	○	○	○	○	○	○
8 glasses of water	○	○	○	○	○	○	○
Meditate	○	○	○	○	○	○	○
Daily journaling	○	○	○	○	○	○	○
Exercise	○	○	○	○	○	○	○
Do something important	○	○	○	○	○	○	○
Do something good	○	○	○	○	○	○	○
Eat healthy	○	○	○	○	○	○	○
Read/listen to something good	○	○	○	○	○	○	○
Connect with others	○	○	○	○	○	○	○

WEEK OF:

MY PRIORITIES FOR THIS WEEK

GRATITUDE LOG:

MAIN GOALS:

DAILY ACTIVITIES

	M	T	W	T	F	S	S
Daily gratitude log	○	○	○	○	○	○	○
Do something fun	○	○	○	○	○	○	○
8 glasses of water	○	○	○	○	○	○	○
Meditate	○	○	○	○	○	○	○
Daily journaling	○	○	○	○	○	○	○
Exercise	○	○	○	○	○	○	○
Do something important	○	○	○	○	○	○	○
Do something good	○	○	○	○	○	○	○
Eat healthy	○	○	○	○	○	○	○
Read/listen to something good	○	○	○	○	○	○	○
Connect with others	○	○	○	○	○	○	○

WEEK OF:

MY PRIORITIES FOR THIS WEEK

GRATITUDE LOG:

MAIN GOALS:

DAILY ACTIVITIES

	M	T	W	T	F	S	S
Daily gratitude log	○	○	○	○	○	○	○
Do something fun	○	○	○	○	○	○	○
8 glasses of water	○	○	○	○	○	○	○
Meditate	○	○	○	○	○	○	○
Daily journaling	○	○	○	○	○	○	○
Exercise	○	○	○	○	○	○	○
Do something important	○	○	○	○	○	○	○
Do something good	○	○	○	○	○	○	○
Eat healthy	○	○	○	○	○	○	○
Read/listen to something good	○	○	○	○	○	○	○
Connect with others	○	○	○	○	○	○	○

WEEK OF:

MY PRIORITIES FOR THIS WEEK

GRATITUDE LOG:

MAIN GOALS:

DAILY ACTIVITIES

M T W T F S S

Daily gratitude log
Do something fun
8 glasses of water
Meditate
Daily journaling
Exercise
Do something important
Do something good
Eat healthy
Read/listen to something good
Connect with others

MY PRIORITIES FOR THIS WEEK

GRATITUDE LOG:

MAIN GOALS:

DAILY ACTIVITIES

	M	T	W	T	F	S	S
Daily gratitude log	○	○	○	○	○	○	○
Do something fun	○	○	○	○	○	○	○
8 glasses of water	○	○	○	○	○	○	○
Meditate	○	○	○	○	○	○	○
Daily journaling	○	○	○	○	○	○	○
Exercise	○	○	○	○	○	○	○
Do something important	○	○	○	○	○	○	○
Do something good	○	○	○	○	○	○	○
Eat healthy	○	○	○	○	○	○	○
Read/listen to something good	○	○	○	○	○	○	○
Connect with others	○	○	○	○	○	○	○

WEEK OF:

MY PRIORITIES FOR THIS WEEK

GRATITUDE LOG:

MAIN GOALS:

DAILY ACTIVITIES

	M	T	W	T	F	S	S
Daily gratitude log	○	○	○	○	○	○	○
Do something fun	○	○	○	○	○	○	○
8 glasses of water	○	○	○	○	○	○	○
Meditate	○	○	○	○	○	○	○
Daily journaling	○	○	○	○	○	○	○
Exercise	○	○	○	○	○	○	○
Do something important	○	○	○	○	○	○	○
Do something good	○	○	○	○	○	○	○
Eat healthy	○	○	○	○	○	○	○
Read/listen to something good	○	○	○	○	○	○	○
Connect with others	○	○	○	○	○	○	○

WEEK OF:

MY PRIORITIES FOR THIS WEEK

GRATITUDE LOG:

MAIN GOALS:

DAILY ACTIVITIES

	M	T	W	T	F	S	S
Daily gratitude log	○	○	○	○	○	○	○
Do something fun	○	○	○	○	○	○	○
8 glasses of water	○	○	○	○	○	○	○
Meditate	○	○	○	○	○	○	○
Daily journaling	○	○	○	○	○	○	○
Exercise	○	○	○	○	○	○	○
Do something important	○	○	○	○	○	○	○
Do something good	○	○	○	○	○	○	○
Eat healthy	○	○	○	○	○	○	○
Read/listen to something good	○	○	○	○	○	○	○
Connect with others	○	○	○	○	○	○	○

WEEK OF:

MY PRIORITIES FOR THIS WEEK

GRATITUDE LOG:

MAIN GOALS:

DAILY ACTIVITIES

M T W T F S S

Daily gratitude log
Do something fun
8 glasses of water
Meditate
Daily journaling
Exercise
Do something
important
Do something good
Eat healthy
Read/listen
to something good
Connect with others

WEEK OF:

MY PRIORITIES FOR THIS WEEK

GRATITUDE LOG:

MAIN GOALS:

DAILY ACTIVITIES

	M	T	W	T	F	S	S
Daily gratitude log	○	○	○	○	○	○	○
Do something fun	○	○	○	○	○	○	○
8 glasses of water	○	○	○	○	○	○	○
Meditate	○	○	○	○	○	○	○
Daily journaling	○	○	○	○	○	○	○
Exercise	○	○	○	○	○	○	○
Do something important	○	○	○	○	○	○	○
Do something good	○	○	○	○	○	○	○
Eat healthy	○	○	○	○	○	○	○
Read/listen to something good	○	○	○	○	○	○	○
Connect with others	○	○	○	○	○	○	○

WEEK OF:

MY PRIORITIES FOR THIS WEEK

GRATITUDE LOG:

MAIN GOALS:

DAILY ACTIVITIES

	M	T	W	T	F	S	S
Daily gratitude log	○	○	○	○	○	○	○
Do something fun	○	○	○	○	○	○	○
8 glasses of water	○	○	○	○	○	○	○
Meditate	○	○	○	○	○	○	○
Daily journaling	○	○	○	○	○	○	○
Exercise	○	○	○	○	○	○	○
Do something important	○	○	○	○	○	○	○
Do something good	○	○	○	○	○	○	○
Eat healthy	○	○	○	○	○	○	○
Read/listen to something good	○	○	○	○	○	○	○
Connect with others	○	○	○	○	○	○	○

MY PRIORITIES FOR THIS WEEK

GRATITUDE LOG:

MAIN GOALS:

DAILY ACTIVITIES

	M	T	W	T	F	S	S
Daily gratitude log	○	○	○	○	○	○	○
Do something fun	○	○	○	○	○	○	○
8 glasses of water	○	○	○	○	○	○	○
Meditate	○	○	○	○	○	○	○
Daily journaling	○	○	○	○	○	○	○
Exercise	○	○	○	○	○	○	○
Do something important	○	○	○	○	○	○	○
Do something good	○	○	○	○	○	○	○
Eat healthy	○	○	○	○	○	○	○
Read/listen to something good	○	○	○	○	○	○	○
Connect with others	○	○	○	○	○	○	○

WEEK OF:

MY PRIORITIES FOR THIS WEEK

GRATITUDE LOG:

MAIN GOALS:

DAILY ACTIVITIES

	M	T	W	T	F	S	S
Daily gratitude log	○	○	○	○	○	○	○
Do something fun	○	○	○	○	○	○	○
8 glasses of water	○	○	○	○	○	○	○
Meditate	○	○	○	○	○	○	○
Daily journaling	○	○	○	○	○	○	○
Exercise	○	○	○	○	○	○	○
Do something important	○	○	○	○	○	○	○
Do something good	○	○	○	○	○	○	○
Eat healthy	○	○	○	○	○	○	○
Read/listen to something good	○	○	○	○	○	○	○
Connect with others	○	○	○	○	○	○	○

MY PRIORITIES FOR THIS WEEK

GRATITUDE LOG:

MAIN GOALS:

DAILY ACTIVITIES

	M	T	W	T	F	S	S
Daily gratitude log	○	○	○	○	○	○	○
Do something fun	○	○	○	○	○	○	○
8 glasses of water	○	○	○	○	○	○	○
Meditate	○	○	○	○	○	○	○
Daily journaling	○	○	○	○	○	○	○
Exercise	○	○	○	○	○	○	○
Do something important	○	○	○	○	○	○	○
Do something good	○	○	○	○	○	○	○
Eat healthy	○	○	○	○	○	○	○
Read/listen to something good	○	○	○	○	○	○	○
Connect with others	○	○	○	○	○	○	○

WEEK OF:

MY PRIORITIES FOR THIS WEEK

GRATITUDE LOG:

MAIN GOALS:

DAILY ACTIVITIES

	M	T	W	T	F	S	S
Daily gratitude log	○	○	○	○	○	○	○
Do something fun	○	○	○	○	○	○	○
8 glasses of water	○	○	○	○	○	○	○
Meditate	○	○	○	○	○	○	○
Daily journaling	○	○	○	○	○	○	○
Exercise	○	○	○	○	○	○	○
Do something important	○	○	○	○	○	○	○
Do something good	○	○	○	○	○	○	○
Eat healthy	○	○	○	○	○	○	○
Read/listen to something good	○	○	○	○	○	○	○
Connect with others	○	○	○	○	○	○	○

MY PRIORITIES FOR THIS WEEK

GRATITUDE LOG:

MAIN GOALS:

DAILY ACTIVITIES

	M	T	W	T	F	S	S
Daily gratitude log	○	○	○	○	○	○	○
Do something fun	○	○	○	○	○	○	○
8 glasses of water	○	○	○	○	○	○	○
Meditate	○	○	○	○	○	○	○
Daily journaling	○	○	○	○	○	○	○
Exercise	○	○	○	○	○	○	○
Do something important	○	○	○	○	○	○	○
Do something good	○	○	○	○	○	○	○
Eat healthy	○	○	○	○	○	○	○
Read/listen to something good	○	○	○	○	○	○	○
Connect with others	○	○	○	○	○	○	○

WEEK OF:

MY PRIORITIES FOR THIS WEEK

GRATITUDE LOG:

MAIN GOALS:

DAILY ACTIVITIES

	M	T	W	T	F	S	S
Daily gratitude log	○	○	○	○	○	○	○
Do something fun	○	○	○	○	○	○	○
8 glasses of water	○	○	○	○	○	○	○
Meditate	○	○	○	○	○	○	○
Daily journaling	○	○	○	○	○	○	○
Exercise	○	○	○	○	○	○	○
Do something important	○	○	○	○	○	○	○
Do something good	○	○	○	○	○	○	○
Eat healthy	○	○	○	○	○	○	○
Read/listen to something good	○	○	○	○	○	○	○
Connect with others	○	○	○	○	○	○	○

MY PRIORITIES FOR THIS WEEK

GRATITUDE LOG:

MAIN GOALS:

DAILY ACTIVITIES

	M	T	W	T	F	S	S
Daily gratitude log	○	○	○	○	○	○	○
Do something fun	○	○	○	○	○	○	○
8 glasses of water	○	○	○	○	○	○	○
Meditate	○	○	○	○	○	○	○
Daily journaling	○	○	○	○	○	○	○
Exercise	○	○	○	○	○	○	○
Do something important	○	○	○	○	○	○	○
Do something good	○	○	○	○	○	○	○
Eat healthy	○	○	○	○	○	○	○
Read/listen to something good	○	○	○	○	○	○	○
Connect with others	○	○	○	○	○	○	○

WEEK OF:

MY PRIORITIES FOR THIS WEEK

GRATITUDE LOG:

MAIN GOALS:

DAILY ACTIVITIES

	M	T	W	T	F	S	S
Daily gratitude log	○	○	○	○	○	○	○
Do something fun	○	○	○	○	○	○	○
8 glasses of water	○	○	○	○	○	○	○
Meditate	○	○	○	○	○	○	○
Daily journaling	○	○	○	○	○	○	○
Exercise	○	○	○	○	○	○	○
Do something important	○	○	○	○	○	○	○
Do something good	○	○	○	○	○	○	○
Eat healthy	○	○	○	○	○	○	○
Read/listen to something good	○	○	○	○	○	○	○
Connect with others	○	○	○	○	○	○	○

live
your
dream.

WEEK OF:

MY PRIORITIES FOR THIS WEEK

GRATITUDE LOG:

MAIN GOALS:

DAILY ACTIVITIES

M T W T F S S

Daily gratitude log
Do something fun
8 glasses of water
Meditate
Daily journaling
Exercise
Do something important
Do something good
Eat healthy
Read/listen to something good
Connect with others

WEEK OF:

MY PRIORITIES FOR THIS WEEK

GRATITUDE LOG:

MAIN GOALS:

DAILY ACTIVITIES

	M	T	W	T	F	S	S
Daily gratitude log	○	○	○	○	○	○	○
Do something fun	○	○	○	○	○	○	○
8 glasses of water	○	○	○	○	○	○	○
Meditate	○	○	○	○	○	○	○
Daily journaling	○	○	○	○	○	○	○
Exercise	○	○	○	○	○	○	○
Do something important	○	○	○	○	○	○	○
Do something good	○	○	○	○	○	○	○
Eat healthy	○	○	○	○	○	○	○
Read/listen to something good	○	○	○	○	○	○	○
Connect with others	○	○	○	○	○	○	○

WEEK OF:

MY PRIORITIES FOR THIS WEEK

GRATITUDE LOG:

MAIN GOALS:

DAILY ACTIVITIES

	M	T	W	T	F	S	S
Daily gratitude log	○	○	○	○	○	○	○
Do something fun	○	○	○	○	○	○	○
8 glasses of water	○	○	○	○	○	○	○
Meditate	○	○	○	○	○	○	○
Daily journaling	○	○	○	○	○	○	○
Exercise	○	○	○	○	○	○	○
Do something important	○	○	○	○	○	○	○
Do something good	○	○	○	○	○	○	○
Eat healthy	○	○	○	○	○	○	○
Read/listen to something good	○	○	○	○	○	○	○
Connect with others	○	○	○	○	○	○	○

WEEK OF:

MY PRIORITIES FOR THIS WEEK

GRATITUDE LOG:

MAIN GOALS:

DAILY ACTIVITIES

M T W T F S S

Daily gratitude log
Do something fun
8 glasses of water
Meditate
Daily journaling
Exercise
Do something
important
Do something good
Eat healthy
Read/listen
to something good
Connect with others

WEEK OF:

MY PRIORITIES FOR THIS WEEK

GRATITUDE LOG:

MAIN GOALS:

DAILY ACTIVITIES

	M	T	W	T	F	S	S
Daily gratitude log	○	○	○	○	○	○	○
Do something fun	○	○	○	○	○	○	○
8 glasses of water	○	○	○	○	○	○	○
Meditate	○	○	○	○	○	○	○
Daily journaling	○	○	○	○	○	○	○
Exercise	○	○	○	○	○	○	○
Do something important	○	○	○	○	○	○	○
Do something good	○	○	○	○	○	○	○
Eat healthy	○	○	○	○	○	○	○
Read/listen to something good	○	○	○	○	○	○	○
Connect with others	○	○	○	○	○	○	○

WEEK OF:

MY PRIORITIES FOR THIS WEEK

GRATITUDE LOG:

MAIN GOALS:

DAILY ACTIVITIES

	M	T	W	T	F	S	S
Daily gratitude log	◯	◯	◯	◯	◯	◯	◯
Do something fun	◯	◯	◯	◯	◯	◯	◯
8 glasses of water	◯	◯	◯	◯	◯	◯	◯
Meditate	◯	◯	◯	◯	◯	◯	◯
Daily journaling	◯	◯	◯	◯	◯	◯	◯
Exercise	◯	◯	◯	◯	◯	◯	◯
Do something important	◯	◯	◯	◯	◯	◯	◯
Do something good	◯	◯	◯	◯	◯	◯	◯
Eat healthy	◯	◯	◯	◯	◯	◯	◯
Read/listen to something good	◯	◯	◯	◯	◯	◯	◯
Connect with others	◯	◯	◯	◯	◯	◯	◯

WEEK OF:

MY PRIORITIES FOR THIS WEEK

GRATITUDE LOG:

MAIN GOALS:

DAILY ACTIVITIES

	M	T	W	T	F	S	S
Daily gratitude log	○	○	○	○	○	○	○
Do something fun	○	○	○	○	○	○	○
8 glasses of water	○	○	○	○	○	○	○
Meditate	○	○	○	○	○	○	○
Daily journaling	○	○	○	○	○	○	○
Exercise	○	○	○	○	○	○	○
Do something important	○	○	○	○	○	○	○
Do something good	○	○	○	○	○	○	○
Eat healthy	○	○	○	○	○	○	○
Read/listen to something good	○	○	○	○	○	○	○
Connect with others	○	○	○	○	○	○	○

WEEK OF:

MY PRIORITIES FOR THIS WEEK

GRATITUDE LOG:

MAIN GOALS:

DAILY ACTIVITIES

	M	T	W	T	F	S	S
Daily gratitude log	○	○	○	○	○	○	○
Do something fun	○	○	○	○	○	○	○
8 glasses of water	○	○	○	○	○	○	○
Meditate	○	○	○	○	○	○	○
Daily journaling	○	○	○	○	○	○	○
Exercise	○	○	○	○	○	○	○
Do something important	○	○	○	○	○	○	○
Do something good	○	○	○	○	○	○	○
Eat healthy	○	○	○	○	○	○	○
Read/listen to something good	○	○	○	○	○	○	○
Connect with others	○	○	○	○	○	○	○

WEEK OF:

MY PRIORITIES FOR THIS WEEK

GRATITUDE LOG:

MAIN GOALS:

DAILY ACTIVITIES

	M	T	W	T	F	S	S
Daily gratitude log	○	○	○	○	○	○	○
Do something fun	○	○	○	○	○	○	○
8 glasses of water	○	○	○	○	○	○	○
Meditate	○	○	○	○	○	○	○
Daily journaling	○	○	○	○	○	○	○
Exercise	○	○	○	○	○	○	○
Do something important	○	○	○	○	○	○	○
Do something good	○	○	○	○	○	○	○
Eat healthy	○	○	○	○	○	○	○
Read/listen to something good	○	○	○	○	○	○	○
Connect with others	○	○	○	○	○	○	○

WEEK OF:

MY PRIORITIES FOR THIS WEEK

GRATITUDE LOG:

MAIN GOALS:

DAILY ACTIVITIES

M T W T F S S

Daily gratitude log
Do something fun
8 glasses of water
Meditate
Daily journaling
Exercise
Do something important
Do something good
Eat healthy
Read/listen to something good
Connect with others

WEEK OF:

MY PRIORITIES FOR THIS WEEK

GRATITUDE LOG:

MAIN GOALS:

DAILY ACTIVITIES

	M	T	W	T	F	S	S
Daily gratitude log	○	○	○	○	○	○	○
Do something fun	○	○	○	○	○	○	○
8 glasses of water	○	○	○	○	○	○	○
Meditate	○	○	○	○	○	○	○
Daily journaling	○	○	○	○	○	○	○
Exercise	○	○	○	○	○	○	○
Do something important	○	○	○	○	○	○	○
Do something good	○	○	○	○	○	○	○
Eat healthy	○	○	○	○	○	○	○
Read/listen to something good	○	○	○	○	○	○	○
Connect with others	○	○	○	○	○	○	○

WEEK OF:

MY PRIORITIES FOR THIS WEEK

GRATITUDE LOG:

MAIN GOALS:

DAILY ACTIVITIES

	M	T	W	T	F	S	S
Daily gratitude log	○	○	○	○	○	○	○
Do something fun	○	○	○	○	○	○	○
8 glasses of water	○	○	○	○	○	○	○
Meditate	○	○	○	○	○	○	○
Daily journaling	○	○	○	○	○	○	○
Exercise	○	○	○	○	○	○	○
Do something important	○	○	○	○	○	○	○
Do something good	○	○	○	○	○	○	○
Eat healthy	○	○	○	○	○	○	○
Read/listen to something good	○	○	○	○	○	○	○
Connect with others	○	○	○	○	○	○	○

WEEK OF:

MY PRIORITIES FOR THIS WEEK

GRATITUDE LOG:

MAIN GOALS:

DAILY ACTIVITIES

M T W T F S S

Daily gratitude log
Do something fun
8 glasses of water
Meditate
Daily journaling
Exercise
Do something
important
Do something good
Eat healthy
Read/listen
to something good
Connect with others

WEEK OF:

MY PRIORITIES FOR THIS WEEK

GRATITUDE LOG:

MAIN GOALS:

DAILY ACTIVITIES

	M	T	W	T	F	S	S
Daily gratitude log	○	○	○	○	○	○	○
Do something fun	○	○	○	○	○	○	○
8 glasses of water	○	○	○	○	○	○	○
Meditate	○	○	○	○	○	○	○
Daily journaling	○	○	○	○	○	○	○
Exercise	○	○	○	○	○	○	○
Do something important	○	○	○	○	○	○	○
Do something good	○	○	○	○	○	○	○
Eat healthy	○	○	○	○	○	○	○
Read/listen to something good	○	○	○	○	○	○	○
Connect with others	○	○	○	○	○	○	○

MY PRIORITIES FOR THIS WEEK

GRATITUDE LOG:

MAIN GOALS:

DAILY ACTIVITIES

	M	T	W	T	F	S	S
Daily gratitude log	○	○	○	○	○	○	○
Do something fun	○	○	○	○	○	○	○
8 glasses of water	○	○	○	○	○	○	○
Meditate	○	○	○	○	○	○	○
Daily journaling	○	○	○	○	○	○	○
Exercise	○	○	○	○	○	○	○
Do something important	○	○	○	○	○	○	○
Do something good	○	○	○	○	○	○	○
Eat healthy	○	○	○	○	○	○	○
Read/listen to something good	○	○	○	○	○	○	○
Connect with others	○	○	○	○	○	○	○

WEEK OF:

MY PRIORITIES FOR THIS WEEK

GRATITUDE LOG:

MAIN GOALS:

DAILY ACTIVITIES

	M	T	W	T	F	S	S
Daily gratitude log	○	○	○	○	○	○	○
Do something fun	○	○	○	○	○	○	○
8 glasses of water	○	○	○	○	○	○	○
Meditate	○	○	○	○	○	○	○
Daily journaling	○	○	○	○	○	○	○
Exercise	○	○	○	○	○	○	○
Do something important	○	○	○	○	○	○	○
Do something good	○	○	○	○	○	○	○
Eat healthy	○	○	○	○	○	○	○
Read/listen to something good	○	○	○	○	○	○	○
Connect with others	○	○	○	○	○	○	○

WEEK OF:

MY PRIORITIES FOR THIS WEEK

GRATITUDE LOG:

MAIN GOALS:

DAILY ACTIVITIES

	M	T	W	T	F	S	S
Daily gratitude log	○	○	○	○	○	○	○
Do something fun	○	○	○	○	○	○	○
8 glasses of water	○	○	○	○	○	○	○
Meditate	○	○	○	○	○	○	○
Daily journaling	○	○	○	○	○	○	○
Exercise	○	○	○	○	○	○	○
Do something important	○	○	○	○	○	○	○
Do something good	○	○	○	○	○	○	○
Eat healthy	○	○	○	○	○	○	○
Read/listen to something good	○	○	○	○	○	○	○
Connect with others	○	○	○	○	○	○	○

MY PRIORITIES FOR THIS WEEK

GRATITUDE LOG:

MAIN GOALS:

DAILY ACTIVITIES

	M	T	W	T	F	S	S
Daily gratitude log	○	○	○	○	○	○	○
Do something fun	○	○	○	○	○	○	○
8 glasses of water	○	○	○	○	○	○	○
Meditate	○	○	○	○	○	○	○
Daily journaling	○	○	○	○	○	○	○
Exercise	○	○	○	○	○	○	○
Do something important	○	○	○	○	○	○	○
Do something good	○	○	○	○	○	○	○
Eat healthy	○	○	○	○	○	○	○
Read/listen to something good	○	○	○	○	○	○	○
Connect with others	○	○	○	○	○	○	○

WEEK OF:

MY PRIORITIES FOR THIS WEEK

GRATITUDE LOG:

MAIN GOALS:

DAILY ACTIVITIES

	M	T	W	T	F	S	S
Daily gratitude log	○	○	○	○	○	○	○
Do something fun	○	○	○	○	○	○	○
8 glasses of water	○	○	○	○	○	○	○
Meditate	○	○	○	○	○	○	○
Daily journaling	○	○	○	○	○	○	○
Exercise	○	○	○	○	○	○	○
Do something important	○	○	○	○	○	○	○
Do something good	○	○	○	○	○	○	○
Eat healthy	○	○	○	○	○	○	○
Read/listen to something good	○	○	○	○	○	○	○
Connect with others	○	○	○	○	○	○	○

WEEK OF:

MY PRIORITIES FOR THIS WEEK

GRATITUDE LOG:

MAIN GOALS:

DAILY ACTIVITIES

	M	T	W	T	F	S	S
Daily gratitude log	○	○	○	○	○	○	○
Do something fun	○	○	○	○	○	○	○
8 glasses of water	○	○	○	○	○	○	○
Meditate	○	○	○	○	○	○	○
Daily journaling	○	○	○	○	○	○	○
Exercise	○	○	○	○	○	○	○
Do something important	○	○	○	○	○	○	○
Do something good	○	○	○	○	○	○	○
Eat healthy	○	○	○	○	○	○	○
Read/listen to something good	○	○	○	○	○	○	○
Connect with others	○	○	○	○	○	○	○

WEEK OF:

MY PRIORITIES FOR THIS WEEK

GRATITUDE LOG:

MAIN GOALS:

DAILY ACTIVITIES

	M	T	W	T	F	S	S
Daily gratitude log	○	○	○	○	○	○	○
Do something fun	○	○	○	○	○	○	○
8 glasses of water	○	○	○	○	○	○	○
Meditate	○	○	○	○	○	○	○
Daily journaling	○	○	○	○	○	○	○
Exercise	○	○	○	○	○	○	○
Do something important	○	○	○	○	○	○	○
Do something good	○	○	○	○	○	○	○
Eat healthy	○	○	○	○	○	○	○
Read/listen to something good	○	○	○	○	○	○	○
Connect with others	○	○	○	○	○	○	○

WEEK OF:

MY PRIORITIES FOR THIS WEEK

GRATITUDE LOG:

MAIN GOALS:

DAILY ACTIVITIES

M T W T F S S

Daily gratitude log
Do something fun
8 glasses of water
Meditate
Daily journaling
Exercise
Do something
important
Do something good
Eat healthy
Read/listen
to something good
Connect with others

WEEK OF:

MY PRIORITIES FOR THIS WEEK

GRATITUDE LOG:

MAIN GOALS:

DAILY ACTIVITIES

	M	T	W	T	F	S	S
Daily gratitude log	○	○	○	○	○	○	○
Do something fun	○	○	○	○	○	○	○
8 glasses of water	○	○	○	○	○	○	○
Meditate	○	○	○	○	○	○	○
Daily journaling	○	○	○	○	○	○	○
Exercise	○	○	○	○	○	○	○
Do something important	○	○	○	○	○	○	○
Do something good	○	○	○	○	○	○	○
Eat healthy	○	○	○	○	○	○	○
Read/listen to something good	○	○	○	○	○	○	○
Connect with others	○	○	○	○	○	○	○

WEEK OF:

MY PRIORITIES FOR THIS WEEK

GRATITUDE LOG:

MAIN GOALS:

DAILY ACTIVITIES

	M	T	W	T	F	S	S
Daily gratitude log	○	○	○	○	○	○	○
Do something fun	○	○	○	○	○	○	○
8 glasses of water	○	○	○	○	○	○	○
Meditate	○	○	○	○	○	○	○
Daily journaling	○	○	○	○	○	○	○
Exercise	○	○	○	○	○	○	○
Do something important	○	○	○	○	○	○	○
Do something good	○	○	○	○	○	○	○
Eat healthy	○	○	○	○	○	○	○
Read/listen to something good	○	○	○	○	○	○	○
Connect with others	○	○	○	○	○	○	○

MY PRIORITIES FOR THIS WEEK

GRATITUDE LOG:

MAIN GOALS:

DAILY ACTIVITIES

	M	T	W	T	F	S	S
Daily gratitude log	○	○	○	○	○	○	○
Do something fun	○	○	○	○	○	○	○
8 glasses of water	○	○	○	○	○	○	○
Meditate	○	○	○	○	○	○	○
Daily journaling	○	○	○	○	○	○	○
Exercise	○	○	○	○	○	○	○
Do something important	○	○	○	○	○	○	○
Do something good	○	○	○	○	○	○	○
Eat healthy	○	○	○	○	○	○	○
Read/listen to something good	○	○	○	○	○	○	○
Connect with others	○	○	○	○	○	○	○

WEEK OF:

MY PRIORITIES FOR THIS WEEK

GRATITUDE LOG:

MAIN GOALS:

DAILY ACTIVITIES

	M	T	W	T	F	S	S
Daily gratitude log	○	○	○	○	○	○	○
Do something fun	○	○	○	○	○	○	○
8 glasses of water	○	○	○	○	○	○	○
Meditate	○	○	○	○	○	○	○
Daily journaling	○	○	○	○	○	○	○
Exercise	○	○	○	○	○	○	○
Do something important	○	○	○	○	○	○	○
Do something good	○	○	○	○	○	○	○
Eat healthy	○	○	○	○	○	○	○
Read/listen to something good	○	○	○	○	○	○	○
Connect with others	○	○	○	○	○	○	○

MY PRIORITIES FOR THIS WEEK

GRATITUDE LOG:

MAIN GOALS:

DAILY ACTIVITIES

	M	T	W	T	F	S	S
Daily gratitude log	○	○	○	○	○	○	○
Do something fun	○	○	○	○	○	○	○
8 glasses of water	○	○	○	○	○	○	○
Meditate	○	○	○	○	○	○	○
Daily journaling	○	○	○	○	○	○	○
Exercise	○	○	○	○	○	○	○
Do something important	○	○	○	○	○	○	○
Do something good	○	○	○	○	○	○	○
Eat healthy	○	○	○	○	○	○	○
Read/listen to something good	○	○	○	○	○	○	○
Connect with others	○	○	○	○	○	○	○

WEEK OF:

MY PRIORITIES FOR THIS WEEK

GRATITUDE LOG:

MAIN GOALS:

DAILY ACTIVITIES

M T W T F S S

Daily gratitude log
Do something fun
8 glasses of water
Meditate
Daily journaling
Exercise
Do something important
Do something good
Eat healthy
Read/listen to something good
Connect with others

WEEK OF:

MY PRIORITIES FOR THIS WEEK

GRATITUDE LOG:

MAIN GOALS:

DAILY ACTIVITIES

M T W T F S S

Daily gratitude log
Do something fun
8 glasses of water
Meditate
Daily journaling
Exercise
Do something important
Do something good
Eat healthy
Read/listen to something good
Connect with others

WEEK OF:

MY PRIORITIES FOR THIS WEEK

GRATITUDE LOG:

MAIN GOALS:

DAILY ACTIVITIES

	M	T	W	T	F	S	S
Daily gratitude log	○	○	○	○	○	○	○
Do something fun	○	○	○	○	○	○	○
8 glasses of water	○	○	○	○	○	○	○
Meditate	○	○	○	○	○	○	○
Daily journaling	○	○	○	○	○	○	○
Exercise	○	○	○	○	○	○	○
Do something important	○	○	○	○	○	○	○
Do something good	○	○	○	○	○	○	○
Eat healthy	○	○	○	○	○	○	○
Read/listen to something good	○	○	○	○	○	○	○
Connect with others	○	○	○	○	○	○	○

WEEK OF:

MY PRIORITIES FOR THIS WEEK

GRATITUDE LOG:

MAIN GOALS:

DAILY ACTIVITIES

	M	T	W	T	F	S	S
Daily gratitude log	○	○	○	○	○	○	○
Do something fun	○	○	○	○	○	○	○
8 glasses of water	○	○	○	○	○	○	○
Meditate	○	○	○	○	○	○	○
Daily journaling	○	○	○	○	○	○	○
Exercise	○	○	○	○	○	○	○
Do something important	○	○	○	○	○	○	○
Do something good	○	○	○	○	○	○	○
Eat healthy	○	○	○	○	○	○	○
Read/listen to something good	○	○	○	○	○	○	○
Connect with others	○	○	○	○	○	○	○

WEEK OF:

MY PRIORITIES FOR THIS WEEK

GRATITUDE LOG:

MAIN GOALS:

DAILY ACTIVITIES

	M	T	W	T	F	S	S
Daily gratitude log	○	○	○	○	○	○	○
Do something fun	○	○	○	○	○	○	○
8 glasses of water	○	○	○	○	○	○	○
Meditate	○	○	○	○	○	○	○
Daily journaling	○	○	○	○	○	○	○
Exercise	○	○	○	○	○	○	○
Do something important	○	○	○	○	○	○	○
Do something good	○	○	○	○	○	○	○
Eat healthy	○	○	○	○	○	○	○
Read/listen to something good	○	○	○	○	○	○	○
Connect with others	○	○	○	○	○	○	○

WEEK OF:

MY PRIORITIES FOR THIS WEEK

GRATITUDE LOG:

MAIN GOALS:

DAILY ACTIVITIES

M T W T F S S

Daily gratitude log
Do something fun
8 glasses of water
Meditate
Daily journaling
Exercise
Do something
important
Do something good
Eat healthy
Read/listen
to something good
Connect with others

MY PRIORITIES FOR THIS WEEK

GRATITUDE LOG:

MAIN GOALS:

DAILY ACTIVITIES

	M	T	W	T	F	S	S
Daily gratitude log	○	○	○	○	○	○	○
Do something fun	○	○	○	○	○	○	○
8 glasses of water	○	○	○	○	○	○	○
Meditate	○	○	○	○	○	○	○
Daily journaling	○	○	○	○	○	○	○
Exercise	○	○	○	○	○	○	○
Do something important	○	○	○	○	○	○	○
Do something good	○	○	○	○	○	○	○
Eat healthy	○	○	○	○	○	○	○
Read/listen to something good	○	○	○	○	○	○	○
Connect with others	○	○	○	○	○	○	○

WEEK OF:

MY PRIORITIES FOR THIS WEEK

GRATITUDE LOG:

MAIN GOALS:

DAILY ACTIVITIES

M T W T F S S

Daily gratitude log
Do something fun
8 glasses of water
Meditate
Daily journaling
Exercise
Do something important
Do something good
Eat healthy
Read/listen to something good
Connect with others

WEEK OF:

MY PRIORITIES FOR THIS WEEK

GRATITUDE LOG:

MAIN GOALS:

DAILY ACTIVITIES

	M	T	W	T	F	S	S
Daily gratitude log	○	○	○	○	○	○	○
Do something fun	○	○	○	○	○	○	○
8 glasses of water	○	○	○	○	○	○	○
Meditate	○	○	○	○	○	○	○
Daily journaling	○	○	○	○	○	○	○
Exercise	○	○	○	○	○	○	○
Do something important	○	○	○	○	○	○	○
Do something good	○	○	○	○	○	○	○
Eat healthy	○	○	○	○	○	○	○
Read/listen to something good	○	○	○	○	○	○	○
Connect with others	○	○	○	○	○	○	○

WEEK OF:

MY PRIORITIES FOR THIS WEEK

GRATITUDE LOG:

MAIN GOALS:

DAILY ACTIVITIES

	M	T	W	T	F	S	S
Daily gratitude log	○	○	○	○	○	○	○
Do something fun	○	○	○	○	○	○	○
8 glasses of water	○	○	○	○	○	○	○
Meditate	○	○	○	○	○	○	○
Daily journaling	○	○	○	○	○	○	○
Exercise	○	○	○	○	○	○	○
Do something important	○	○	○	○	○	○	○
Do something good	○	○	○	○	○	○	○
Eat healthy	○	○	○	○	○	○	○
Read/listen to something good	○	○	○	○	○	○	○
Connect with others	○	○	○	○	○	○	○

WEEK OF:

MY PRIORITIES FOR THIS WEEK

GRATITUDE LOG:

MAIN GOALS:

DAILY ACTIVITIES

	M	T	W	T	F	S	S
Daily gratitude log	○	○	○	○	○	○	○
Do something fun	○	○	○	○	○	○	○
8 glasses of water	○	○	○	○	○	○	○
Meditate	○	○	○	○	○	○	○
Daily journaling	○	○	○	○	○	○	○
Exercise	○	○	○	○	○	○	○
Do something important	○	○	○	○	○	○	○
Do something good	○	○	○	○	○	○	○
Eat healthy	○	○	○	○	○	○	○
Read/listen to something good	○	○	○	○	○	○	○
Connect with others	○	○	○	○	○	○	○

WEEK OF:

MY PRIORITIES FOR THIS WEEK

GRATITUDE LOG:

MAIN GOALS:

DAILY ACTIVITIES

	M	T	W	T	F	S	S
Daily gratitude log	○	○	○	○	○	○	○
Do something fun	○	○	○	○	○	○	○
8 glasses of water	○	○	○	○	○	○	○
Meditate	○	○	○	○	○	○	○
Daily journaling	○	○	○	○	○	○	○
Exercise	○	○	○	○	○	○	○
Do something important	○	○	○	○	○	○	○
Do something good	○	○	○	○	○	○	○
Eat healthy	○	○	○	○	○	○	○
Read/listen to something good	○	○	○	○	○	○	○
Connect with others	○	○	○	○	○	○	○

WEEK OF:

MY PRIORITIES FOR THIS WEEK

GRATITUDE LOG: MAIN GOALS:

DAILY ACTIVITIES

	M	T	W	T	F	S	S
Daily gratitude log	○	○	○	○	○	○	○
Do something fun	○	○	○	○	○	○	○
8 glasses of water	○	○	○	○	○	○	○
Meditate	○	○	○	○	○	○	○
Daily journaling	○	○	○	○	○	○	○
Exercise	○	○	○	○	○	○	○
Do something important	○	○	○	○	○	○	○
Do something good	○	○	○	○	○	○	○
Eat healthy	○	○	○	○	○	○	○
Read/listen to something good	○	○	○	○	○	○	○
Connect with others	○	○	○	○	○	○	○

WEEK OF:

MY PRIORITIES FOR THIS WEEK

GRATITUDE LOG:

MAIN GOALS:

DAILY ACTIVITIES

M T W T F S S

Daily gratitude log
Do something fun
8 glasses of water
Meditate
Daily journaling
Exercise
Do something
important
Do something good
Eat healthy
Read/listen
to something good
Connect with others

WEEK OF:

MY PRIORITIES FOR THIS WEEK

GRATITUDE LOG:

MAIN GOALS:

DAILY ACTIVITIES

	M	T	W	T	F	S	S
Daily gratitude log	○	○	○	○	○	○	○
Do something fun	○	○	○	○	○	○	○
8 glasses of water	○	○	○	○	○	○	○
Meditate	○	○	○	○	○	○	○
Daily journaling	○	○	○	○	○	○	○
Exercise	○	○	○	○	○	○	○
Do something important	○	○	○	○	○	○	○
Do something good	○	○	○	○	○	○	○
Eat healthy	○	○	○	○	○	○	○
Read/listen to something good	○	○	○	○	○	○	○
Connect with others	○	○	○	○	○	○	○

WEEK OF:

MY PRIORITIES FOR THIS WEEK

GRATITUDE LOG:

MAIN GOALS:

DAILY ACTIVITIES

M T W T F S S

Daily gratitude log
Do something fun
8 glasses of water
Meditate
Daily journaling
Exercise
Do something important
Do something good
Eat healthy
Read/listen to something good
Connect with others

WEEK OF:

MY PRIORITIES FOR THIS WEEK

GRATITUDE LOG:

MAIN GOALS:

DAILY ACTIVITIES

M T W T F S S

Daily gratitude log
Do something fun
8 glasses of water
Meditate
Daily journaling
Exercise
Do something
important
Do something good
Eat healthy
Read/listen
to something good
Connect with others

WEEK OF:

MY PRIORITIES FOR THIS WEEK

GRATITUDE LOG:

MAIN GOALS:

DAILY ACTIVITIES

M T W T F S S

Daily gratitude log
Do something fun
8 glasses of water
Meditate
Daily journaling
Exercise
Do something
important
Do something good
Eat healthy
Read/listen
to something good
Connect with others

MY PRIORITIES FOR THIS WEEK

GRATITUDE LOG:

MAIN GOALS:

DAILY ACTIVITIES

	M	T	W	T	F	S	S
Daily gratitude log	○	○	○	○	○	○	○
Do something fun	○	○	○	○	○	○	○
8 glasses of water	○	○	○	○	○	○	○
Meditate	○	○	○	○	○	○	○
Daily journaling	○	○	○	○	○	○	○
Exercise	○	○	○	○	○	○	○
Do something important	○	○	○	○	○	○	○
Do something good	○	○	○	○	○	○	○
Eat healthy	○	○	○	○	○	○	○
Read/listen to something good	○	○	○	○	○	○	○
Connect with others	○	○	○	○	○	○	○

WEEK OF:

MY PRIORITIES FOR THIS WEEK

GRATITUDE LOG:

MAIN GOALS:

DAILY ACTIVITIES

	M	T	W	T	F	S	S
Daily gratitude log	○	○	○	○	○	○	○
Do something fun	○	○	○	○	○	○	○
8 glasses of water	○	○	○	○	○	○	○
Meditate	○	○	○	○	○	○	○
Daily journaling	○	○	○	○	○	○	○
Exercise	○	○	○	○	○	○	○
Do something important	○	○	○	○	○	○	○
Do something good	○	○	○	○	○	○	○
Eat healthy	○	○	○	○	○	○	○
Read/listen to something good	○	○	○	○	○	○	○
Connect with others	○	○	○	○	○	○	○

WEEK OF:

MY PRIORITIES FOR THIS WEEK

GRATITUDE LOG:

MAIN GOALS:

DAILY ACTIVITIES

	M	T	W	T	F	S	S
Daily gratitude log	○	○	○	○	○	○	○
Do something fun	○	○	○	○	○	○	○
8 glasses of water	○	○	○	○	○	○	○
Meditate	○	○	○	○	○	○	○
Daily journaling	○	○	○	○	○	○	○
Exercise	○	○	○	○	○	○	○
Do something important	○	○	○	○	○	○	○
Do something good	○	○	○	○	○	○	○
Eat healthy	○	○	○	○	○	○	○
Read/listen to something good	○	○	○	○	○	○	○
Connect with others	○	○	○	○	○	○	○

WEEK OF:

MY PRIORITIES FOR THIS WEEK

✏️

GRATITUDE LOG:

MAIN GOALS:

DAILY ACTIVITIES

	M	T	W	T	F	S	S
Daily gratitude log	○	○	○	○	○	○	○
Do something fun	○	○	○	○	○	○	○
8 glasses of water	○	○	○	○	○	○	○
Meditate	○	○	○	○	○	○	○
Daily journaling	○	○	○	○	○	○	○
Exercise	○	○	○	○	○	○	○
Do something important	○	○	○	○	○	○	○
Do something good	○	○	○	○	○	○	○
Eat healthy	○	○	○	○	○	○	○
Read/listen to something good	○	○	○	○	○	○	○
Connect with others	○	○	○	○	○	○	○

WEEK OF:

MY PRIORITIES FOR THIS WEEK

GRATITUDE LOG:

MAIN GOALS:

DAILY ACTIVITIES

	M	T	W	T	F	S	S
Daily gratitude log	○	○	○	○	○	○	○
Do something fun	○	○	○	○	○	○	○
8 glasses of water	○	○	○	○	○	○	○
Meditate	○	○	○	○	○	○	○
Daily journaling	○	○	○	○	○	○	○
Exercise	○	○	○	○	○	○	○
Do something important	○	○	○	○	○	○	○
Do something good	○	○	○	○	○	○	○
Eat healthy	○	○	○	○	○	○	○
Read/listen to something good	○	○	○	○	○	○	○
Connect with others	○	○	○	○	○	○	○

WEEK OF:

MY PRIORITIES FOR THIS WEEK

GRATITUDE LOG:

MAIN GOALS:

DAILY ACTIVITIES

M T W T F S S

Daily gratitude log
Do something fun
8 glasses of water
Meditate
Daily journaling
Exercise
Do something important
Do something good
Eat healthy
Read/listen to something good
Connect with others

WEEK OF:

MY PRIORITIES FOR THIS WEEK

GRATITUDE LOG:

MAIN GOALS:

DAILY ACTIVITIES

	M	T	W	T	F	S	S
Daily gratitude log	○	○	○	○	○	○	○
Do something fun	○	○	○	○	○	○	○
8 glasses of water	○	○	○	○	○	○	○
Meditate	○	○	○	○	○	○	○
Daily journaling	○	○	○	○	○	○	○
Exercise	○	○	○	○	○	○	○
Do something important	○	○	○	○	○	○	○
Do something good	○	○	○	○	○	○	○
Eat healthy	○	○	○	○	○	○	○
Read/listen to something good	○	○	○	○	○	○	○
Connect with others	○	○	○	○	○	○	○

live
your
dream.

WEEK OF:

MY PRIORITIES FOR THIS WEEK

GRATITUDE LOG:

MAIN GOALS:

DAILY ACTIVITIES

	M	T	W	T	F	S	S
Daily gratitude log	○	○	○	○	○	○	○
Do something fun	○	○	○	○	○	○	○
8 glasses of water	○	○	○	○	○	○	○
Meditate	○	○	○	○	○	○	○
Daily journaling	○	○	○	○	○	○	○
Exercise	○	○	○	○	○	○	○
Do something important	○	○	○	○	○	○	○
Do something good	○	○	○	○	○	○	○
Eat healthy	○	○	○	○	○	○	○
Read/listen to something good	○	○	○	○	○	○	○
Connect with others	○	○	○	○	○	○	○

WEEK OF:

MY PRIORITIES FOR THIS WEEK

GRATITUDE LOG:

MAIN GOALS:

DAILY ACTIVITIES

	M	T	W	T	F	S	S
Daily gratitude log	○	○	○	○	○	○	○
Do something fun	○	○	○	○	○	○	○
8 glasses of water	○	○	○	○	○	○	○
Meditate	○	○	○	○	○	○	○
Daily journaling	○	○	○	○	○	○	○
Exercise	○	○	○	○	○	○	○
Do something important	○	○	○	○	○	○	○
Do something good	○	○	○	○	○	○	○
Eat healthy	○	○	○	○	○	○	○
Read/listen to something good	○	○	○	○	○	○	○
Connect with others	○	○	○	○	○	○	○

WEEK OF:

MY PRIORITIES FOR THIS WEEK

GRATITUDE LOG:

MAIN GOALS:

DAILY ACTIVITIES

	M	T	W	T	F	S	S
Daily gratitude log	○	○	○	○	○	○	○
Do something fun	○	○	○	○	○	○	○
8 glasses of water	○	○	○	○	○	○	○
Meditate	○	○	○	○	○	○	○
Daily journaling	○	○	○	○	○	○	○
Exercise	○	○	○	○	○	○	○
Do something important	○	○	○	○	○	○	○
Do something good	○	○	○	○	○	○	○
Eat healthy	○	○	○	○	○	○	○
Read/listen to something good	○	○	○	○	○	○	○
Connect with others	○	○	○	○	○	○	○

MY PRIORITIES FOR THIS WEEK

GRATITUDE LOG:

MAIN GOALS:

DAILY ACTIVITIES

	M	T	W	T	F	S	S
Daily gratitude log	○	○	○	○	○	○	○
Do something fun	○	○	○	○	○	○	○
8 glasses of water	○	○	○	○	○	○	○
Meditate	○	○	○	○	○	○	○
Daily journaling	○	○	○	○	○	○	○
Exercise	○	○	○	○	○	○	○
Do something important	○	○	○	○	○	○	○
Do something good	○	○	○	○	○	○	○
Eat healthy	○	○	○	○	○	○	○
Read/listen to something good	○	○	○	○	○	○	○
Connect with others	○	○	○	○	○	○	○

WEEK OF:

MY PRIORITIES FOR THIS WEEK

GRATITUDE LOG:

MAIN GOALS:

DAILY ACTIVITIES

M T W T F S S

Daily gratitude log
Do something fun
8 glasses of water
Meditate
Daily journaling
Exercise
Do something important
Do something good
Eat healthy
Read/listen to something good
Connect with others

WEEK OF:

MY PRIORITIES FOR THIS WEEK

GRATITUDE LOG:

MAIN GOALS:

DAILY ACTIVITIES

M T W T F S S

Daily gratitude log
Do something fun
8 glasses of water
Meditate
Daily journaling
Exercise
Do something important
Do something good
Eat healthy
Read/listen to something good
Connect with others

MY PRIORITIES FOR THIS WEEK

GRATITUDE LOG:

MAIN GOALS:

DAILY ACTIVITIES

	M	T	W	T	F	S	S
Daily gratitude log	○	○	○	○	○	○	○
Do something fun	○	○	○	○	○	○	○
8 glasses of water	○	○	○	○	○	○	○
Meditate	○	○	○	○	○	○	○
Daily journaling	○	○	○	○	○	○	○
Exercise	○	○	○	○	○	○	○
Do something important	○	○	○	○	○	○	○
Do something good	○	○	○	○	○	○	○
Eat healthy	○	○	○	○	○	○	○
Read/listen to something good	○	○	○	○	○	○	○
Connect with others	○	○	○	○	○	○	○

WEEK OF:

MY PRIORITIES FOR THIS WEEK

GRATITUDE LOG:

MAIN GOALS:

DAILY ACTIVITIES

	M	T	W	T	F	S	S
Daily gratitude log	○	○	○	○	○	○	○
Do something fun	○	○	○	○	○	○	○
8 glasses of water	○	○	○	○	○	○	○
Meditate	○	○	○	○	○	○	○
Daily journaling	○	○	○	○	○	○	○
Exercise	○	○	○	○	○	○	○
Do something important	○	○	○	○	○	○	○
Do something good	○	○	○	○	○	○	○
Eat healthy	○	○	○	○	○	○	○
Read/listen to something good	○	○	○	○	○	○	○
Connect with others	○	○	○	○	○	○	○

WEEK OF:

MY PRIORITIES FOR THIS WEEK

GRATITUDE LOG:

MAIN GOALS:

DAILY ACTIVITIES

	M	T	W	T	F	S	S
Daily gratitude log	○	○	○	○	○	○	○
Do something fun	○	○	○	○	○	○	○
8 glasses of water	○	○	○	○	○	○	○
Meditate	○	○	○	○	○	○	○
Daily journaling	○	○	○	○	○	○	○
Exercise	○	○	○	○	○	○	○
Do something important	○	○	○	○	○	○	○
Do something good	○	○	○	○	○	○	○
Eat healthy	○	○	○	○	○	○	○
Read/listen to something good	○	○	○	○	○	○	○
Connect with others	○	○	○	○	○	○	○

MY PRIORITIES FOR THIS WEEK

GRATITUDE LOG:

MAIN GOALS:

DAILY ACTIVITIES

	M	T	W	T	F	S	S
Daily gratitude log	○	○	○	○	○	○	○
Do something fun	○	○	○	○	○	○	○
8 glasses of water	○	○	○	○	○	○	○
Meditate	○	○	○	○	○	○	○
Daily journaling	○	○	○	○	○	○	○
Exercise	○	○	○	○	○	○	○
Do something important	○	○	○	○	○	○	○
Do something good	○	○	○	○	○	○	○
Eat healthy	○	○	○	○	○	○	○
Read/listen to something good	○	○	○	○	○	○	○
Connect with others	○	○	○	○	○	○	○

WEEK OF:

MY PRIORITIES FOR THIS WEEK

GRATITUDE LOG:

MAIN GOALS:

DAILY ACTIVITIES

	M	T	W	T	F	S	S
Daily gratitude log	◯	◯	◯	◯	◯	◯	◯
Do something fun	◯	◯	◯	◯	◯	◯	◯
8 glasses of water	◯	◯	◯	◯	◯	◯	◯
Meditate	◯	◯	◯	◯	◯	◯	◯
Daily journaling	◯	◯	◯	◯	◯	◯	◯
Exercise	◯	◯	◯	◯	◯	◯	◯
Do something important	◯	◯	◯	◯	◯	◯	◯
Do something good	◯	◯	◯	◯	◯	◯	◯
Eat healthy	◯	◯	◯	◯	◯	◯	◯
Read/listen to something good	◯	◯	◯	◯	◯	◯	◯
Connect with others	◯	◯	◯	◯	◯	◯	◯

WEEK OF:

MY PRIORITIES FOR THIS WEEK

GRATITUDE LOG:

MAIN GOALS:

DAILY ACTIVITIES

M T W T F S S

Daily gratitude log
Do something fun
8 glasses of water
Meditate
Daily journaling
Exercise
Do something important
Do something good
Eat healthy
Read/listen to something good
Connect with others

WEEK OF:

MY PRIORITIES FOR THIS WEEK

GRATITUDE LOG:

MAIN GOALS:

DAILY ACTIVITIES

	M	T	W	T	F	S	S
Daily gratitude log	○	○	○	○	○	○	○
Do something fun	○	○	○	○	○	○	○
8 glasses of water	○	○	○	○	○	○	○
Meditate	○	○	○	○	○	○	○
Daily journaling	○	○	○	○	○	○	○
Exercise	○	○	○	○	○	○	○
Do something important	○	○	○	○	○	○	○
Do something good	○	○	○	○	○	○	○
Eat healthy	○	○	○	○	○	○	○
Read/listen to something good	○	○	○	○	○	○	○
Connect with others	○	○	○	○	○	○	○

WEEK OF:

MY PRIORITIES FOR THIS WEEK

GRATITUDE LOG:

MAIN GOALS:

DAILY ACTIVITIES

	M	T	W	T	F	S	S
Daily gratitude log	○	○	○	○	○	○	○
Do something fun	○	○	○	○	○	○	○
8 glasses of water	○	○	○	○	○	○	○
Meditate	○	○	○	○	○	○	○
Daily journaling	○	○	○	○	○	○	○
Exercise	○	○	○	○	○	○	○
Do something important	○	○	○	○	○	○	○
Do something good	○	○	○	○	○	○	○
Eat healthy	○	○	○	○	○	○	○
Read/listen to something good	○	○	○	○	○	○	○
Connect with others	○	○	○	○	○	○	○

WEEK OF:

MY PRIORITIES FOR THIS WEEK

GRATITUDE LOG:

MAIN GOALS:

DAILY ACTIVITIES

	M	T	W	T	F	S	S
Daily gratitude log	○	○	○	○	○	○	○
Do something fun	○	○	○	○	○	○	○
8 glasses of water	○	○	○	○	○	○	○
Meditate	○	○	○	○	○	○	○
Daily journaling	○	○	○	○	○	○	○
Exercise	○	○	○	○	○	○	○
Do something important	○	○	○	○	○	○	○
Do something good	○	○	○	○	○	○	○
Eat healthy	○	○	○	○	○	○	○
Read/listen to something good	○	○	○	○	○	○	○
Connect with others	○	○	○	○	○	○	○

MY PRIORITIES FOR THIS WEEK

GRATITUDE LOG:

MAIN GOALS:

DAILY ACTIVITIES

	M	T	W	T	F	S	S
Daily gratitude log	○	○	○	○	○	○	○
Do something fun	○	○	○	○	○	○	○
8 glasses of water	○	○	○	○	○	○	○
Meditate	○	○	○	○	○	○	○
Daily journaling	○	○	○	○	○	○	○
Exercise	○	○	○	○	○	○	○
Do something important	○	○	○	○	○	○	○
Do something good	○	○	○	○	○	○	○
Eat healthy	○	○	○	○	○	○	○
Read/listen to something good	○	○	○	○	○	○	○
Connect with others	○	○	○	○	○	○	○

WEEK OF:

MY PRIORITIES FOR THIS WEEK

GRATITUDE LOG:

MAIN GOALS:

DAILY ACTIVITIES

	M	T	W	T	F	S	S
Daily gratitude log	○	○	○	○	○	○	○
Do something fun	○	○	○	○	○	○	○
8 glasses of water	○	○	○	○	○	○	○
Meditate	○	○	○	○	○	○	○
Daily journaling	○	○	○	○	○	○	○
Exercise	○	○	○	○	○	○	○
Do something important	○	○	○	○	○	○	○
Do something good	○	○	○	○	○	○	○
Eat healthy	○	○	○	○	○	○	○
Read/listen to something good	○	○	○	○	○	○	○
Connect with others	○	○	○	○	○	○	○

WEEK OF:

MY PRIORITIES FOR THIS WEEK

GRATITUDE LOG:

MAIN GOALS:

DAILY ACTIVITIES

M T W T F S S

Daily gratitude log
Do something fun
8 glasses of water
Meditate
Daily journaling
Exercise
Do something important
Do something good
Eat healthy
Read/listen to something good
Connect with others

WEEK OF:

MY PRIORITIES FOR THIS WEEK

GRATITUDE LOG:

MAIN GOALS:

DAILY ACTIVITIES

	M	T	W	T	F	S	S
Daily gratitude log	○	○	○	○	○	○	○
Do something fun	○	○	○	○	○	○	○
8 glasses of water	○	○	○	○	○	○	○
Meditate	○	○	○	○	○	○	○
Daily journaling	○	○	○	○	○	○	○
Exercise	○	○	○	○	○	○	○
Do something important	○	○	○	○	○	○	○
Do something good	○	○	○	○	○	○	○
Eat healthy	○	○	○	○	○	○	○
Read/listen to something good	○	○	○	○	○	○	○
Connect with others	○	○	○	○	○	○	○

WEEK OF:

MY PRIORITIES FOR THIS WEEK

GRATITUDE LOG:

MAIN GOALS:

DAILY ACTIVITIES

	M	T	W	T	F	S	S
Daily gratitude log	○	○	○	○	○	○	○
Do something fun	○	○	○	○	○	○	○
8 glasses of water	○	○	○	○	○	○	○
Meditate	○	○	○	○	○	○	○
Daily journaling	○	○	○	○	○	○	○
Exercise	○	○	○	○	○	○	○
Do something important	○	○	○	○	○	○	○
Do something good	○	○	○	○	○	○	○
Eat healthy	○	○	○	○	○	○	○
Read/listen to something good	○	○	○	○	○	○	○
Connect with others	○	○	○	○	○	○	○

WEEK OF:

MY PRIORITIES FOR THIS WEEK

GRATITUDE LOG:

MAIN GOALS:

DAILY ACTIVITIES

	M	T	W	T	F	S	S
Daily gratitude log	○	○	○	○	○	○	○
Do something fun	○	○	○	○	○	○	○
8 glasses of water	○	○	○	○	○	○	○
Meditate	○	○	○	○	○	○	○
Daily journaling	○	○	○	○	○	○	○
Exercise	○	○	○	○	○	○	○
Do something important	○	○	○	○	○	○	○
Do something good	○	○	○	○	○	○	○
Eat healthy	○	○	○	○	○	○	○
Read/listen to something good	○	○	○	○	○	○	○
Connect with others	○	○	○	○	○	○	○

WEEK OF:

MY PRIORITIES FOR THIS WEEK

GRATITUDE LOG:

MAIN GOALS:

DAILY ACTIVITIES

	M	T	W	T	F	S	S
Daily gratitude log	○	○	○	○	○	○	○
Do something fun	○	○	○	○	○	○	○
8 glasses of water	○	○	○	○	○	○	○
Meditate	○	○	○	○	○	○	○
Daily journaling	○	○	○	○	○	○	○
Exercise	○	○	○	○	○	○	○
Do something important	○	○	○	○	○	○	○
Do something good	○	○	○	○	○	○	○
Eat healthy	○	○	○	○	○	○	○
Read/listen to something good	○	○	○	○	○	○	○
Connect with others	○	○	○	○	○	○	○

WEEK OF:

MY PRIORITIES FOR THIS WEEK

GRATITUDE LOG:

MAIN GOALS:

DAILY ACTIVITIES

	M	T	W	T	F	S	S
Daily gratitude log	○	○	○	○	○	○	○
Do something fun	○	○	○	○	○	○	○
8 glasses of water	○	○	○	○	○	○	○
Meditate	○	○	○	○	○	○	○
Daily journaling	○	○	○	○	○	○	○
Exercise	○	○	○	○	○	○	○
Do something important	○	○	○	○	○	○	○
Do something good	○	○	○	○	○	○	○
Eat healthy	○	○	○	○	○	○	○
Read/listen to something good	○	○	○	○	○	○	○
Connect with others	○	○	○	○	○	○	○

MY PRIORITIES FOR THIS WEEK

GRATITUDE LOG:

MAIN GOALS:

DAILY ACTIVITIES

	M	T	W	T	F	S	S
Daily gratitude log	○	○	○	○	○	○	○
Do something fun	○	○	○	○	○	○	○
8 glasses of water	○	○	○	○	○	○	○
Meditate	○	○	○	○	○	○	○
Daily journaling	○	○	○	○	○	○	○
Exercise	○	○	○	○	○	○	○
Do something important	○	○	○	○	○	○	○
Do something good	○	○	○	○	○	○	○
Eat healthy	○	○	○	○	○	○	○
Read/listen to something good	○	○	○	○	○	○	○
Connect with others	○	○	○	○	○	○	○

WEEK OF:

MY PRIORITIES FOR THIS WEEK

GRATITUDE LOG:

MAIN GOALS:

DAILY ACTIVITIES

	M	T	W	T	F	S	S
Daily gratitude log	○	○	○	○	○	○	○
Do something fun	○	○	○	○	○	○	○
8 glasses of water	○	○	○	○	○	○	○
Meditate	○	○	○	○	○	○	○
Daily journaling	○	○	○	○	○	○	○
Exercise	○	○	○	○	○	○	○
Do something important	○	○	○	○	○	○	○
Do something good	○	○	○	○	○	○	○
Eat healthy	○	○	○	○	○	○	○
Read/listen to something good	○	○	○	○	○	○	○
Connect with others	○	○	○	○	○	○	○

MY PRIORITIES FOR THIS WEEK

GRATITUDE LOG:

MAIN GOALS:

DAILY ACTIVITIES

	M	T	W	T	F	S	S
Daily gratitude log	○	○	○	○	○	○	○
Do something fun	○	○	○	○	○	○	○
8 glasses of water	○	○	○	○	○	○	○
Meditate	○	○	○	○	○	○	○
Daily journaling	○	○	○	○	○	○	○
Exercise	○	○	○	○	○	○	○
Do something important	○	○	○	○	○	○	○
Do something good	○	○	○	○	○	○	○
Eat healthy	○	○	○	○	○	○	○
Read/listen to something good	○	○	○	○	○	○	○
Connect with others	○	○	○	○	○	○	○

MY PRIORITIES FOR THIS WEEK

GRATITUDE LOG:

MAIN GOALS:

DAILY ACTIVITIES

	M	T	W	T	F	S	S
Daily gratitude log	○	○	○	○	○	○	○
Do something fun	○	○	○	○	○	○	○
8 glasses of water	○	○	○	○	○	○	○
Meditate	○	○	○	○	○	○	○
Daily journaling	○	○	○	○	○	○	○
Exercise	○	○	○	○	○	○	○
Do something important	○	○	○	○	○	○	○
Do something good	○	○	○	○	○	○	○
Eat healthy	○	○	○	○	○	○	○
Read/listen to something good	○	○	○	○	○	○	○
Connect with others	○	○	○	○	○	○	○

WEEK OF:

MY PRIORITIES FOR THIS WEEK

GRATITUDE LOG:

MAIN GOALS:

DAILY ACTIVITIES

	M	T	W	T	F	S	S
Daily gratitude log	○	○	○	○	○	○	○
Do something fun	○	○	○	○	○	○	○
8 glasses of water	○	○	○	○	○	○	○
Meditate	○	○	○	○	○	○	○
Daily journaling	○	○	○	○	○	○	○
Exercise	○	○	○	○	○	○	○
Do something important	○	○	○	○	○	○	○
Do something good	○	○	○	○	○	○	○
Eat healthy	○	○	○	○	○	○	○
Read/listen to something good	○	○	○	○	○	○	○
Connect with others	○	○	○	○	○	○	○

WEEK OF:

MY PRIORITIES FOR THIS WEEK

GRATITUDE LOG:

MAIN GOALS:

DAILY ACTIVITIES

M T W T F S S

Daily gratitude log
Do something fun
8 glasses of water
Meditate
Daily journaling
Exercise
Do something important
Do something good
Eat healthy
Read/listen to something good
Connect with others

WEEK OF:

MY PRIORITIES FOR THIS WEEK

GRATITUDE LOG:

MAIN GOALS:

DAILY ACTIVITIES

	M	T	W	T	F	S	S
Daily gratitude log	○	○	○	○	○	○	○
Do something fun	○	○	○	○	○	○	○
8 glasses of water	○	○	○	○	○	○	○
Meditate	○	○	○	○	○	○	○
Daily journaling	○	○	○	○	○	○	○
Exercise	○	○	○	○	○	○	○
Do something important	○	○	○	○	○	○	○
Do something good	○	○	○	○	○	○	○
Eat healthy	○	○	○	○	○	○	○
Read/listen to something good	○	○	○	○	○	○	○
Connect with others	○	○	○	○	○	○	○

WEEK OF:

MY PRIORITIES FOR THIS WEEK

GRATITUDE LOG:

MAIN GOALS:

DAILY ACTIVITIES

	M	T	W	T	F	S	S
Daily gratitude log	○	○	○	○	○	○	○
Do something fun	○	○	○	○	○	○	○
8 glasses of water	○	○	○	○	○	○	○
Meditate	○	○	○	○	○	○	○
Daily journaling	○	○	○	○	○	○	○
Exercise	○	○	○	○	○	○	○
Do something important	○	○	○	○	○	○	○
Do something good	○	○	○	○	○	○	○
Eat healthy	○	○	○	○	○	○	○
Read/listen to something good	○	○	○	○	○	○	○
Connect with others	○	○	○	○	○	○	○

WEEK OF:

MY PRIORITIES FOR THIS WEEK

GRATITUDE LOG:

MAIN GOALS:

DAILY ACTIVITIES

	M	T	W	T	F	S	S
Daily gratitude log	○	○	○	○	○	○	○
Do something fun	○	○	○	○	○	○	○
8 glasses of water	○	○	○	○	○	○	○
Meditate	○	○	○	○	○	○	○
Daily journaling	○	○	○	○	○	○	○
Exercise	○	○	○	○	○	○	○
Do something important	○	○	○	○	○	○	○
Do something good	○	○	○	○	○	○	○
Eat healthy	○	○	○	○	○	○	○
Read/listen to something good	○	○	○	○	○	○	○
Connect with others	○	○	○	○	○	○	○

WEEK OF:

MY PRIORITIES FOR THIS WEEK

GRATITUDE LOG:

MAIN GOALS:

DAILY ACTIVITIES

M T W T F S S

Daily gratitude log
Do something fun
8 glasses of water
Meditate
Daily journaling
Exercise
Do something
important
Do something good
Eat healthy
Read/listen
to something good
Connect with others

MY PRIORITIES FOR THIS WEEK

GRATITUDE LOG:

MAIN GOALS:

DAILY ACTIVITIES

	M	T	W	T	F	S	S
Daily gratitude log	○	○	○	○	○	○	○
Do something fun	○	○	○	○	○	○	○
8 glasses of water	○	○	○	○	○	○	○
Meditate	○	○	○	○	○	○	○
Daily journaling	○	○	○	○	○	○	○
Exercise	○	○	○	○	○	○	○
Do something important	○	○	○	○	○	○	○
Do something good	○	○	○	○	○	○	○
Eat healthy	○	○	○	○	○	○	○
Read/listen to something good	○	○	○	○	○	○	○
Connect with others	○	○	○	○	○	○	○

WEEK OF:

MY PRIORITIES FOR THIS WEEK

GRATITUDE LOG:

MAIN GOALS:

DAILY ACTIVITIES

	M	T	W	T	F	S	S
Daily gratitude log	○	○	○	○	○	○	○
Do something fun	○	○	○	○	○	○	○
8 glasses of water	○	○	○	○	○	○	○
Meditate	○	○	○	○	○	○	○
Daily journaling	○	○	○	○	○	○	○
Exercise	○	○	○	○	○	○	○
Do something important	○	○	○	○	○	○	○
Do something good	○	○	○	○	○	○	○
Eat healthy	○	○	○	○	○	○	○
Read/listen to something good	○	○	○	○	○	○	○
Connect with others	○	○	○	○	○	○	○

DAILY ACTIVITIES

	M	T	W	T	F	S	S
Daily gratitude log	○	○	○	○	○	○	○
Do something fun	○	○	○	○	○	○	○
8 glasses of water	○	○	○	○	○	○	○
Meditate	○	○	○	○	○	○	○
Daily journaling	○	○	○	○	○	○	○
Exercise	○	○	○	○	○	○	○
Do something important	○	○	○	○	○	○	○
Do something good	○	○	○	○	○	○	○
Eat healthy	○	○	○	○	○	○	○
Read/listen to something good	○	○	○	○	○	○	○
Connect with others	○	○	○	○	○	○	○

WEEK OF:

MY PRIORITIES FOR THIS WEEK

GRATITUDE LOG:

MAIN GOALS:

DAILY ACTIVITIES

	M	T	W	T	F	S	S
Daily gratitude log	○	○	○	○	○	○	○
Do something fun	○	○	○	○	○	○	○
8 glasses of water	○	○	○	○	○	○	○
Meditate	○	○	○	○	○	○	○
Daily journaling	○	○	○	○	○	○	○
Exercise	○	○	○	○	○	○	○
Do something important	○	○	○	○	○	○	○
Do something good	○	○	○	○	○	○	○
Eat healthy	○	○	○	○	○	○	○
Read/listen to something good	○	○	○	○	○	○	○
Connect with others	○	○	○	○	○	○	○

WEEK OF:

MY PRIORITIES FOR THIS WEEK

GRATITUDE LOG:

MAIN GOALS:

DAILY ACTIVITIES

	M	T	W	T	F	S	S
Daily gratitude log	○	○	○	○	○	○	○
Do something fun	○	○	○	○	○	○	○
8 glasses of water	○	○	○	○	○	○	○
Meditate	○	○	○	○	○	○	○
Daily journaling	○	○	○	○	○	○	○
Exercise	○	○	○	○	○	○	○
Do something important	○	○	○	○	○	○	○
Do something good	○	○	○	○	○	○	○
Eat healthy	○	○	○	○	○	○	○
Read/listen to something good	○	○	○	○	○	○	○
Connect with others	○	○	○	○	○	○	○

WEEK OF:

MY PRIORITIES FOR THIS WEEK

GRATITUDE LOG:

MAIN GOALS:

DAILY ACTIVITIES

	M	T	W	T	F	S	S
Daily gratitude log	○	○	○	○	○	○	○
Do something fun	○	○	○	○	○	○	○
8 glasses of water	○	○	○	○	○	○	○
Meditate	○	○	○	○	○	○	○
Daily journaling	○	○	○	○	○	○	○
Exercise	○	○	○	○	○	○	○
Do something important	○	○	○	○	○	○	○
Do something good	○	○	○	○	○	○	○
Eat healthy	○	○	○	○	○	○	○
Read/listen to something good	○	○	○	○	○	○	○
Connect with others	○	○	○	○	○	○	○

MY PRIORITIES FOR THIS WEEK

GRATITUDE LOG:

MAIN GOALS:

DAILY ACTIVITIES

	M	T	W	T	F	S	S
Daily gratitude log	○	○	○	○	○	○	○
Do something fun	○	○	○	○	○	○	○
8 glasses of water	○	○	○	○	○	○	○
Meditate	○	○	○	○	○	○	○
Daily journaling	○	○	○	○	○	○	○
Exercise	○	○	○	○	○	○	○
Do something important	○	○	○	○	○	○	○
Do something good	○	○	○	○	○	○	○
Eat healthy	○	○	○	○	○	○	○
Read/listen to something good	○	○	○	○	○	○	○
Connect with others	○	○	○	○	○	○	○

MY PRIORITIES FOR THIS WEEK

GRATITUDE LOG:

MAIN GOALS:

DAILY ACTIVITIES

	M	T	W	T	F	S	S
Daily gratitude log	○	○	○	○	○	○	○
Do something fun	○	○	○	○	○	○	○
8 glasses of water	○	○	○	○	○	○	○
Meditate	○	○	○	○	○	○	○
Daily journaling	○	○	○	○	○	○	○
Exercise	○	○	○	○	○	○	○
Do something important	○	○	○	○	○	○	○
Do something good	○	○	○	○	○	○	○
Eat healthy	○	○	○	○	○	○	○
Read/listen to something good	○	○	○	○	○	○	○
Connect with others	○	○	○	○	○	○	○

WEEK OF:

MY PRIORITIES FOR THIS WEEK

GRATITUDE LOG:

MAIN GOALS:

DAILY ACTIVITIES

	M	T	W	T	F	S	S
Daily gratitude log	○	○	○	○	○	○	○
Do something fun	○	○	○	○	○	○	○
8 glasses of water	○	○	○	○	○	○	○
Meditate	○	○	○	○	○	○	○
Daily journaling	○	○	○	○	○	○	○
Exercise	○	○	○	○	○	○	○
Do something important	○	○	○	○	○	○	○
Do something good	○	○	○	○	○	○	○
Eat healthy	○	○	○	○	○	○	○
Read/listen to something good	○	○	○	○	○	○	○
Connect with others	○	○	○	○	○	○	○

WEEK OF:

MY PRIORITIES FOR THIS WEEK

GRATITUDE LOG:

MAIN GOALS:

DAILY ACTIVITIES

	M	T	W	T	F	S	S
Daily gratitude log	○	○	○	○	○	○	○
Do something fun	○	○	○	○	○	○	○
8 glasses of water	○	○	○	○	○	○	○
Meditate	○	○	○	○	○	○	○
Daily journaling	○	○	○	○	○	○	○
Exercise	○	○	○	○	○	○	○
Do something important	○	○	○	○	○	○	○
Do something good	○	○	○	○	○	○	○
Eat healthy	○	○	○	○	○	○	○
Read/listen to something good	○	○	○	○	○	○	○
Connect with others	○	○	○	○	○	○	○

WEEK OF:

MY PRIORITIES FOR THIS WEEK

GRATITUDE LOG:

MAIN GOALS:

DAILY ACTIVITIES

	M	T	W	T	F	S	S
Daily gratitude log	○	○	○	○	○	○	○
Do something fun	○	○	○	○	○	○	○
8 glasses of water	○	○	○	○	○	○	○
Meditate	○	○	○	○	○	○	○
Daily journaling	○	○	○	○	○	○	○
Exercise	○	○	○	○	○	○	○
Do something important	○	○	○	○	○	○	○
Do something good	○	○	○	○	○	○	○
Eat healthy	○	○	○	○	○	○	○
Read/listen to something good	○	○	○	○	○	○	○
Connect with others	○	○	○	○	○	○	○

WEEK OF:

MY PRIORITIES FOR THIS WEEK

GRATITUDE LOG:

MAIN GOALS:

DAILY ACTIVITIES

M T W T F S S

Daily gratitude log
Do something fun
8 glasses of water
Meditate
Daily journaling
Exercise
Do something important
Do something good
Eat healthy
Read/listen to something good
Connect with others

MY PRIORITIES FOR THIS WEEK

GRATITUDE LOG:

MAIN GOALS:

DAILY ACTIVITIES

	M	T	W	T	F	S	S
Daily gratitude log	○	○	○	○	○	○	○
Do something fun	○	○	○	○	○	○	○
8 glasses of water	○	○	○	○	○	○	○
Meditate	○	○	○	○	○	○	○
Daily journaling	○	○	○	○	○	○	○
Exercise	○	○	○	○	○	○	○
Do something important	○	○	○	○	○	○	○
Do something good	○	○	○	○	○	○	○
Eat healthy	○	○	○	○	○	○	○
Read/listen to something good	○	○	○	○	○	○	○
Connect with others	○	○	○	○	○	○	○

WEEK OF:

MY PRIORITIES FOR THIS WEEK

GRATITUDE LOG:

MAIN GOALS:

DAILY ACTIVITIES

	M	T	W	T	F	S	S
Daily gratitude log	○	○	○	○	○	○	○
Do something fun	○	○	○	○	○	○	○
8 glasses of water	○	○	○	○	○	○	○
Meditate	○	○	○	○	○	○	○
Daily journaling	○	○	○	○	○	○	○
Exercise	○	○	○	○	○	○	○
Do something important	○	○	○	○	○	○	○
Do something good	○	○	○	○	○	○	○
Eat healthy	○	○	○	○	○	○	○
Read/listen to something good	○	○	○	○	○	○	○
Connect with others	○	○	○	○	○	○	○

MY PRIORITIES FOR THIS WEEK

GRATITUDE LOG:

MAIN GOALS:

DAILY ACTIVITIES

	M	T	W	T	F	S	S
Daily gratitude log	○	○	○	○	○	○	○
Do something fun	○	○	○	○	○	○	○
8 glasses of water	○	○	○	○	○	○	○
Meditate	○	○	○	○	○	○	○
Daily journaling	○	○	○	○	○	○	○
Exercise	○	○	○	○	○	○	○
Do something important	○	○	○	○	○	○	○
Do something good	○	○	○	○	○	○	○
Eat healthy	○	○	○	○	○	○	○
Read/listen to something good	○	○	○	○	○	○	○
Connect with others	○	○	○	○	○	○	○

WEEK OF:

MY PRIORITIES FOR THIS WEEK

GRATITUDE LOG:

MAIN GOALS:

DAILY ACTIVITIES

	M	T	W	T	F	S	S
Daily gratitude log	○	○	○	○	○	○	○
Do something fun	○	○	○	○	○	○	○
8 glasses of water	○	○	○	○	○	○	○
Meditate	○	○	○	○	○	○	○
Daily journaling	○	○	○	○	○	○	○
Exercise	○	○	○	○	○	○	○
Do something important	○	○	○	○	○	○	○
Do something good	○	○	○	○	○	○	○
Eat healthy	○	○	○	○	○	○	○
Read/listen to something good	○	○	○	○	○	○	○
Connect with others	○	○	○	○	○	○	○

MY PRIORITIES FOR THIS WEEK

GRATITUDE LOG:

MAIN GOALS:

DAILY ACTIVITIES

	M	T	W	T	F	S	S
Daily gratitude log	○	○	○	○	○	○	○
Do something fun	○	○	○	○	○	○	○
8 glasses of water	○	○	○	○	○	○	○
Meditate	○	○	○	○	○	○	○
Daily journaling	○	○	○	○	○	○	○
Exercise	○	○	○	○	○	○	○
Do something important	○	○	○	○	○	○	○
Do something good	○	○	○	○	○	○	○
Eat healthy	○	○	○	○	○	○	○
Read/listen to something good	○	○	○	○	○	○	○
Connect with others	○	○	○	○	○	○	○

MY PRIORITIES FOR THIS WEEK

GRATITUDE LOG:

MAIN GOALS:

DAILY ACTIVITIES

	M	T	W	T	F	S	S
Daily gratitude log	○	○	○	○	○	○	○
Do something fun	○	○	○	○	○	○	○
8 glasses of water	○	○	○	○	○	○	○
Meditate	○	○	○	○	○	○	○
Daily journaling	○	○	○	○	○	○	○
Exercise	○	○	○	○	○	○	○
Do something important	○	○	○	○	○	○	○
Do something good	○	○	○	○	○	○	○
Eat healthy	○	○	○	○	○	○	○
Read/listen to something good	○	○	○	○	○	○	○
Connect with others	○	○	○	○	○	○	○

MY PRIORITIES FOR THIS WEEK

GRATITUDE LOG:

MAIN GOALS:

DAILY ACTIVITIES

	M	T	W	T	F	S	S
Daily gratitude log	○	○	○	○	○	○	○
Do something fun	○	○	○	○	○	○	○
8 glasses of water	○	○	○	○	○	○	○
Meditate	○	○	○	○	○	○	○
Daily journaling	○	○	○	○	○	○	○
Exercise	○	○	○	○	○	○	○
Do something important	○	○	○	○	○	○	○
Do something good	○	○	○	○	○	○	○
Eat healthy	○	○	○	○	○	○	○
Read/listen to something good	○	○	○	○	○	○	○
Connect with others	○	○	○	○	○	○	○

live
your
dream.

WEEK OF:

MY PRIORITIES FOR THIS WEEK

GRATITUDE LOG:

MAIN GOALS:

DAILY ACTIVITIES

	M	T	W	T	F	S	S
Daily gratitude log	○	○	○	○	○	○	○
Do something fun	○	○	○	○	○	○	○
8 glasses of water	○	○	○	○	○	○	○
Meditate	○	○	○	○	○	○	○
Daily journaling	○	○	○	○	○	○	○
Exercise	○	○	○	○	○	○	○
Do something important	○	○	○	○	○	○	○
Do something good	○	○	○	○	○	○	○
Eat healthy	○	○	○	○	○	○	○
Read/listen to something good	○	○	○	○	○	○	○
Connect with others	○	○	○	○	○	○	○

WEEK OF:

MY PRIORITIES FOR THIS WEEK

GRATITUDE LOG:

MAIN GOALS:

DAILY ACTIVITIES

	M	T	W	T	F	S	S
Daily gratitude log	○	○	○	○	○	○	○
Do something fun	○	○	○	○	○	○	○
8 glasses of water	○	○	○	○	○	○	○
Meditate	○	○	○	○	○	○	○
Daily journaling	○	○	○	○	○	○	○
Exercise	○	○	○	○	○	○	○
Do something important	○	○	○	○	○	○	○
Do something good	○	○	○	○	○	○	○
Eat healthy	○	○	○	○	○	○	○
Read/listen to something good	○	○	○	○	○	○	○
Connect with others	○	○	○	○	○	○	○

WEEK OF:

MY PRIORITIES FOR THIS WEEK

GRATITUDE LOG:

MAIN GOALS:

DAILY ACTIVITIES

	M	T	W	T	F	S	S
Daily gratitude log	○	○	○	○	○	○	○
Do something fun	○	○	○	○	○	○	○
8 glasses of water	○	○	○	○	○	○	○
Meditate	○	○	○	○	○	○	○
Daily journaling	○	○	○	○	○	○	○
Exercise	○	○	○	○	○	○	○
Do something important	○	○	○	○	○	○	○
Do something good	○	○	○	○	○	○	○
Eat healthy	○	○	○	○	○	○	○
Read/listen to something good	○	○	○	○	○	○	○
Connect with others	○	○	○	○	○	○	○

WEEK OF:

MY PRIORITIES FOR THIS WEEK

GRATITUDE LOG:

MAIN GOALS:

DAILY ACTIVITIES

	M	T	W	T	F	S	S
Daily gratitude log	○	○	○	○	○	○	○
Do something fun	○	○	○	○	○	○	○
8 glasses of water	○	○	○	○	○	○	○
Meditate	○	○	○	○	○	○	○
Daily journaling	○	○	○	○	○	○	○
Exercise	○	○	○	○	○	○	○
Do something important	○	○	○	○	○	○	○
Do something good	○	○	○	○	○	○	○
Eat healthy	○	○	○	○	○	○	○
Read/listen to something good	○	○	○	○	○	○	○
Connect with others	○	○	○	○	○	○	○

WEEK OF:

MY PRIORITIES FOR THIS WEEK

GRATITUDE LOG:

MAIN GOALS:

DAILY ACTIVITIES

M T W T F S S

Daily gratitude log
Do something fun
8 glasses of water
Meditate
Daily journaling
Exercise
Do something
important
Do something good
Eat healthy
Read/listen
to something good
Connect with others

MY PRIORITIES FOR THIS WEEK

GRATITUDE LOG:

MAIN GOALS:

DAILY ACTIVITIES

	M	T	W	T	F	S	S
Daily gratitude log	○	○	○	○	○	○	○
Do something fun	○	○	○	○	○	○	○
8 glasses of water	○	○	○	○	○	○	○
Meditate	○	○	○	○	○	○	○
Daily journaling	○	○	○	○	○	○	○
Exercise	○	○	○	○	○	○	○
Do something important	○	○	○	○	○	○	○
Do something good	○	○	○	○	○	○	○
Eat healthy	○	○	○	○	○	○	○
Read/listen to something good	○	○	○	○	○	○	○
Connect with others	○	○	○	○	○	○	○

WEEK OF:

MY PRIORITIES FOR THIS WEEK

GRATITUDE LOG:

MAIN GOALS:

DAILY ACTIVITIES

	M	T	W	T	F	S	S
Daily gratitude log	○	○	○	○	○	○	○
Do something fun	○	○	○	○	○	○	○
8 glasses of water	○	○	○	○	○	○	○
Meditate	○	○	○	○	○	○	○
Daily journaling	○	○	○	○	○	○	○
Exercise	○	○	○	○	○	○	○
Do something important	○	○	○	○	○	○	○
Do something good	○	○	○	○	○	○	○
Eat healthy	○	○	○	○	○	○	○
Read/listen to something good	○	○	○	○	○	○	○
Connect with others	○	○	○	○	○	○	○

MY PRIORITIES FOR THIS WEEK

GRATITUDE LOG:

MAIN GOALS:

DAILY ACTIVITIES

	M	T	W	T	F	S	S
Daily gratitude log	○	○	○	○	○	○	○
Do something fun	○	○	○	○	○	○	○
8 glasses of water	○	○	○	○	○	○	○
Meditate	○	○	○	○	○	○	○
Daily journaling	○	○	○	○	○	○	○
Exercise	○	○	○	○	○	○	○
Do something important	○	○	○	○	○	○	○
Do something good	○	○	○	○	○	○	○
Eat healthy	○	○	○	○	○	○	○
Read/listen to something good	○	○	○	○	○	○	○
Connect with others	○	○	○	○	○	○	○

WEEK OF:

MY PRIORITIES FOR THIS WEEK

GRATITUDE LOG:

MAIN GOALS:

DAILY ACTIVITIES

M T W T F S S

Daily gratitude log
Do something fun
8 glasses of water
Meditate
Daily journaling
Exercise
Do something
important
Do something good
Eat healthy
Read/listen
to something good
Connect with others

WEEK OF:

MY PRIORITIES FOR THIS WEEK

GRATITUDE LOG:

MAIN GOALS:

DAILY ACTIVITIES

	M	T	W	T	F	S	S
Daily gratitude log	○	○	○	○	○	○	○
Do something fun	○	○	○	○	○	○	○
8 glasses of water	○	○	○	○	○	○	○
Meditate	○	○	○	○	○	○	○
Daily journaling	○	○	○	○	○	○	○
Exercise	○	○	○	○	○	○	○
Do something important	○	○	○	○	○	○	○
Do something good	○	○	○	○	○	○	○
Eat healthy	○	○	○	○	○	○	○
Read/listen to something good	○	○	○	○	○	○	○
Connect with others	○	○	○	○	○	○	○

MY PRIORITIES FOR THIS WEEK

GRATITUDE LOG:

MAIN GOALS:

DAILY ACTIVITIES

	M	T	W	T	F	S	S
Daily gratitude log	○	○	○	○	○	○	○
Do something fun	○	○	○	○	○	○	○
8 glasses of water	○	○	○	○	○	○	○
Meditate	○	○	○	○	○	○	○
Daily journaling	○	○	○	○	○	○	○
Exercise	○	○	○	○	○	○	○
Do something important	○	○	○	○	○	○	○
Do something good	○	○	○	○	○	○	○
Eat healthy	○	○	○	○	○	○	○
Read/listen to something good	○	○	○	○	○	○	○
Connect with others	○	○	○	○	○	○	○

WEEK OF:

MY PRIORITIES FOR THIS WEEK

GRATITUDE LOG:

MAIN GOALS:

DAILY ACTIVITIES

	M	T	W	T	F	S	S
Daily gratitude log	○	○	○	○	○	○	○
Do something fun	○	○	○	○	○	○	○
8 glasses of water	○	○	○	○	○	○	○
Meditate	○	○	○	○	○	○	○
Daily journaling	○	○	○	○	○	○	○
Exercise	○	○	○	○	○	○	○
Do something important	○	○	○	○	○	○	○
Do something good	○	○	○	○	○	○	○
Eat healthy	○	○	○	○	○	○	○
Read/listen to something good	○	○	○	○	○	○	○
Connect with others	○	○	○	○	○	○	○

WEEK OF:

MY PRIORITIES FOR THIS WEEK

GRATITUDE LOG:

MAIN GOALS:

DAILY ACTIVITIES

	M	T	W	T	F	S	S
Daily gratitude log	○	○	○	○	○	○	○
Do something fun	○	○	○	○	○	○	○
8 glasses of water	○	○	○	○	○	○	○
Meditate	○	○	○	○	○	○	○
Daily journaling	○	○	○	○	○	○	○
Exercise	○	○	○	○	○	○	○
Do something important	○	○	○	○	○	○	○
Do something good	○	○	○	○	○	○	○
Eat healthy	○	○	○	○	○	○	○
Read/listen to something good	○	○	○	○	○	○	○
Connect with others	○	○	○	○	○	○	○

WEEK OF:

MY PRIORITIES FOR THIS WEEK

GRATITUDE LOG:

MAIN GOALS:

DAILY ACTIVITIES

	M	T	W	T	F	S	S
Daily gratitude log	○	○	○	○	○	○	○
Do something fun	○	○	○	○	○	○	○
8 glasses of water	○	○	○	○	○	○	○
Meditate	○	○	○	○	○	○	○
Daily journaling	○	○	○	○	○	○	○
Exercise	○	○	○	○	○	○	○
Do something important	○	○	○	○	○	○	○
Do something good	○	○	○	○	○	○	○
Eat healthy	○	○	○	○	○	○	○
Read/listen to something good	○	○	○	○	○	○	○
Connect with others	○	○	○	○	○	○	○

WEEK OF:

MY PRIORITIES FOR THIS WEEK

GRATITUDE LOG:

MAIN GOALS:

DAILY ACTIVITIES

M T W T F S S

Daily gratitude log
Do something fun
8 glasses of water
Meditate
Daily journaling
Exercise
Do something
important
Do something good
Eat healthy
Read/listen
to something good
Connect with others

WEEK OF:

MY PRIORITIES FOR THIS WEEK

GRATITUDE LOG:

MAIN GOALS:

DAILY ACTIVITIES

	M	T	W	T	F	S	S
Daily gratitude log	○	○	○	○	○	○	○
Do something fun	○	○	○	○	○	○	○
8 glasses of water	○	○	○	○	○	○	○
Meditate	○	○	○	○	○	○	○
Daily journaling	○	○	○	○	○	○	○
Exercise	○	○	○	○	○	○	○
Do something important	○	○	○	○	○	○	○
Do something good	○	○	○	○	○	○	○
Eat healthy	○	○	○	○	○	○	○
Read/listen to something good	○	○	○	○	○	○	○
Connect with others	○	○	○	○	○	○	○

MY PRIORITIES FOR THIS WEEK

GRATITUDE LOG:

MAIN GOALS:

DAILY ACTIVITIES

	M	T	W	T	F	S	S
Daily gratitude log	○	○	○	○	○	○	○
Do something fun	○	○	○	○	○	○	○
8 glasses of water	○	○	○	○	○	○	○
Meditate	○	○	○	○	○	○	○
Daily journaling	○	○	○	○	○	○	○
Exercise	○	○	○	○	○	○	○
Do something important	○	○	○	○	○	○	○
Do something good	○	○	○	○	○	○	○
Eat healthy	○	○	○	○	○	○	○
Read/listen to something good	○	○	○	○	○	○	○
Connect with others	○	○	○	○	○	○	○

MY PRIORITIES FOR THIS WEEK

GRATITUDE LOG:

MAIN GOALS:

DAILY ACTIVITIES

	M	T	W	T	F	S	S
Daily gratitude log	○	○	○	○	○	○	○
Do something fun	○	○	○	○	○	○	○
8 glasses of water	○	○	○	○	○	○	○
Meditate	○	○	○	○	○	○	○
Daily journaling	○	○	○	○	○	○	○
Exercise	○	○	○	○	○	○	○
Do something important	○	○	○	○	○	○	○
Do something good	○	○	○	○	○	○	○
Eat healthy	○	○	○	○	○	○	○
Read/listen to something good	○	○	○	○	○	○	○
Connect with others	○	○	○	○	○	○	○

MY PRIORITIES FOR THIS WEEK

GRATITUDE LOG:

MAIN GOALS:

DAILY ACTIVITIES

	M	T	W	T	F	S	S
Daily gratitude log	○	○	○	○	○	○	○
Do something fun	○	○	○	○	○	○	○
8 glasses of water	○	○	○	○	○	○	○
Meditate	○	○	○	○	○	○	○
Daily journaling	○	○	○	○	○	○	○
Exercise	○	○	○	○	○	○	○
Do something important	○	○	○	○	○	○	○
Do something good	○	○	○	○	○	○	○
Eat healthy	○	○	○	○	○	○	○
Read/listen to something good	○	○	○	○	○	○	○
Connect with others	○	○	○	○	○	○	○

WEEK OF:

MY PRIORITIES FOR THIS WEEK

GRATITUDE LOG:

MAIN GOALS:

DAILY ACTIVITIES

M T W T F S S

Daily gratitude log
Do something fun
8 glasses of water
Meditate
Daily journaling
Exercise
Do something
important
Do something good
Eat healthy
Read/listen
to something good
Connect with others

WEEK OF:

MY PRIORITIES FOR THIS WEEK

GRATITUDE LOG:

MAIN GOALS:

DAILY ACTIVITIES

	M	T	W	T	F	S	S
Daily gratitude log	○	○	○	○	○	○	○
Do something fun	○	○	○	○	○	○	○
8 glasses of water	○	○	○	○	○	○	○
Meditate	○	○	○	○	○	○	○
Daily journaling	○	○	○	○	○	○	○
Exercise	○	○	○	○	○	○	○
Do something important	○	○	○	○	○	○	○
Do something good	○	○	○	○	○	○	○
Eat healthy	○	○	○	○	○	○	○
Read/listen to something good	○	○	○	○	○	○	○
Connect with others	○	○	○	○	○	○	○

WEEK OF:

MY PRIORITIES FOR THIS WEEK

GRATITUDE LOG:

MAIN GOALS:

DAILY ACTIVITIES

	M	T	W	T	F	S	S
Daily gratitude log	○	○	○	○	○	○	○
Do something fun	○	○	○	○	○	○	○
8 glasses of water	○	○	○	○	○	○	○
Meditate	○	○	○	○	○	○	○
Daily journaling	○	○	○	○	○	○	○
Exercise	○	○	○	○	○	○	○
Do something important	○	○	○	○	○	○	○
Do something good	○	○	○	○	○	○	○
Eat healthy	○	○	○	○	○	○	○
Read/listen to something good	○	○	○	○	○	○	○
Connect with others	○	○	○	○	○	○	○

WEEK OF:

MY PRIORITIES FOR THIS WEEK

GRATITUDE LOG:

MAIN GOALS:

DAILY ACTIVITIES

	M	T	W	T	F	S	S
Daily gratitude log	○	○	○	○	○	○	○
Do something fun	○	○	○	○	○	○	○
8 glasses of water	○	○	○	○	○	○	○
Meditate	○	○	○	○	○	○	○
Daily journaling	○	○	○	○	○	○	○
Exercise	○	○	○	○	○	○	○
Do something important	○	○	○	○	○	○	○
Do something good	○	○	○	○	○	○	○
Eat healthy	○	○	○	○	○	○	○
Read/listen to something good	○	○	○	○	○	○	○
Connect with others	○	○	○	○	○	○	○

MY PRIORITIES FOR THIS WEEK

GRATITUDE LOG:

MAIN GOALS:

DAILY ACTIVITIES

	M	T	W	T	F	S	S
Daily gratitude log	○	○	○	○	○	○	○
Do something fun	○	○	○	○	○	○	○
8 glasses of water	○	○	○	○	○	○	○
Meditate	○	○	○	○	○	○	○
Daily journaling	○	○	○	○	○	○	○
Exercise	○	○	○	○	○	○	○
Do something important	○	○	○	○	○	○	○
Do something good	○	○	○	○	○	○	○
Eat healthy	○	○	○	○	○	○	○
Read/listen to something good	○	○	○	○	○	○	○
Connect with others	○	○	○	○	○	○	○

WEEK OF:

MY PRIORITIES FOR THIS WEEK

GRATITUDE LOG:

MAIN GOALS:

DAILY ACTIVITIES

	M	T	W	T	F	S	S
Daily gratitude log	○	○	○	○	○	○	○
Do something fun	○	○	○	○	○	○	○
8 glasses of water	○	○	○	○	○	○	○
Meditate	○	○	○	○	○	○	○
Daily journaling	○	○	○	○	○	○	○
Exercise	○	○	○	○	○	○	○
Do something important	○	○	○	○	○	○	○
Do something good	○	○	○	○	○	○	○
Eat healthy	○	○	○	○	○	○	○
Read/listen to something good	○	○	○	○	○	○	○
Connect with others	○	○	○	○	○	○	○

WEEK OF:

MY PRIORITIES FOR THIS WEEK

GRATITUDE LOG:

MAIN GOALS:

DAILY ACTIVITIES

	M	T	W	T	F	S	S
Daily gratitude log	○	○	○	○	○	○	○
Do something fun	○	○	○	○	○	○	○
8 glasses of water	○	○	○	○	○	○	○
Meditate	○	○	○	○	○	○	○
Daily journaling	○	○	○	○	○	○	○
Exercise	○	○	○	○	○	○	○
Do something important	○	○	○	○	○	○	○
Do something good	○	○	○	○	○	○	○
Eat healthy	○	○	○	○	○	○	○
Read/listen to something good	○	○	○	○	○	○	○
Connect with others	○	○	○	○	○	○	○

WEEK OF:

MY PRIORITIES FOR THIS WEEK

GRATITUDE LOG:

MAIN GOALS:

DAILY ACTIVITIES

M T W T F S S

Daily gratitude log
Do something fun
8 glasses of water
Meditate
Daily journaling
Exercise
Do something important
Do something good
Eat healthy
Read/listen to something good
Connect with others

WEEK OF:

MY PRIORITIES FOR THIS WEEK

GRATITUDE LOG:

MAIN GOALS:

DAILY ACTIVITIES

	M	T	W	T	F	S	S
Daily gratitude log	○	○	○	○	○	○	○
Do something fun	○	○	○	○	○	○	○
8 glasses of water	○	○	○	○	○	○	○
Meditate	○	○	○	○	○	○	○
Daily journaling	○	○	○	○	○	○	○
Exercise	○	○	○	○	○	○	○
Do something important	○	○	○	○	○	○	○
Do something good	○	○	○	○	○	○	○
Eat healthy	○	○	○	○	○	○	○
Read/listen to something good	○	○	○	○	○	○	○
Connect with others	○	○	○	○	○	○	○

WEEK OF:

MY PRIORITIES FOR THIS WEEK

GRATITUDE LOG:

MAIN GOALS:

DAILY ACTIVITIES

M T W T F S S

Daily gratitude log
Do something fun
8 glasses of water
Meditate
Daily journaling
Exercise
Do something
important
Do something good
Eat healthy
Read/listen
to something good
Connect with others

WEEK OF:

MY PRIORITIES FOR THIS WEEK

GRATITUDE LOG:

MAIN GOALS:

DAILY ACTIVITIES

	M	T	W	T	F	S	S
Daily gratitude log	○	○	○	○	○	○	○
Do something fun	○	○	○	○	○	○	○
8 glasses of water	○	○	○	○	○	○	○
Meditate	○	○	○	○	○	○	○
Daily journaling	○	○	○	○	○	○	○
Exercise	○	○	○	○	○	○	○
Do something important	○	○	○	○	○	○	○
Do something good	○	○	○	○	○	○	○
Eat healthy	○	○	○	○	○	○	○
Read/listen to something good	○	○	○	○	○	○	○
Connect with others	○	○	○	○	○	○	○

WEEK OF:

MY PRIORITIES FOR THIS WEEK

GRATITUDE LOG:

MAIN GOALS:

DAILY ACTIVITIES

M T W T F S S

Daily gratitude log
Do something fun
8 glasses of water
Meditate
Daily journaling
Exercise
Do something important
Do something good
Eat healthy
Read/listen to something good
Connect with others

WEEK OF:

MY PRIORITIES FOR THIS WEEK

GRATITUDE LOG:

MAIN GOALS:

DAILY ACTIVITIES

	M	T	W	T	F	S	S
Daily gratitude log	○	○	○	○	○	○	○
Do something fun	○	○	○	○	○	○	○
8 glasses of water	○	○	○	○	○	○	○
Meditate	○	○	○	○	○	○	○
Daily journaling	○	○	○	○	○	○	○
Exercise	○	○	○	○	○	○	○
Do something important	○	○	○	○	○	○	○
Do something good	○	○	○	○	○	○	○
Eat healthy	○	○	○	○	○	○	○
Read/listen to something good	○	○	○	○	○	○	○
Connect with others	○	○	○	○	○	○	○

WEEK OF:

MY PRIORITIES FOR THIS WEEK

GRATITUDE LOG:

MAIN GOALS:

DAILY ACTIVITIES

	M	T	W	T	F	S	S
Daily gratitude log	○	○	○	○	○	○	○
Do something fun	○	○	○	○	○	○	○
8 glasses of water	○	○	○	○	○	○	○
Meditate	○	○	○	○	○	○	○
Daily journaling	○	○	○	○	○	○	○
Exercise	○	○	○	○	○	○	○
Do something important	○	○	○	○	○	○	○
Do something good	○	○	○	○	○	○	○
Eat healthy	○	○	○	○	○	○	○
Read/listen to something good	○	○	○	○	○	○	○
Connect with others	○	○	○	○	○	○	○

WEEK OF:

MY PRIORITIES FOR THIS WEEK

GRATITUDE LOG:

MAIN GOALS:

DAILY ACTIVITIES

M T W T F S S

Daily gratitude log
Do something fun
8 glasses of water
Meditate
Daily journaling
Exercise
Do something
important
Do something good
Eat healthy
Read/listen
to something good
Connect with others

MY PRIORITIES FOR THIS WEEK

GRATITUDE LOG:

MAIN GOALS:

DAILY ACTIVITIES

	M	T	W	T	F	S	S
Daily gratitude log	○	○	○	○	○	○	○
Do something fun	○	○	○	○	○	○	○
8 glasses of water	○	○	○	○	○	○	○
Meditate	○	○	○	○	○	○	○
Daily journaling	○	○	○	○	○	○	○
Exercise	○	○	○	○	○	○	○
Do something important	○	○	○	○	○	○	○
Do something good	○	○	○	○	○	○	○
Eat healthy	○	○	○	○	○	○	○
Read/listen to something good	○	○	○	○	○	○	○
Connect with others	○	○	○	○	○	○	○

WEEK OF:

MY PRIORITIES FOR THIS WEEK

GRATITUDE LOG:

MAIN GOALS:

DAILY ACTIVITIES

M T W T F S S

Daily gratitude log
Do something fun
8 glasses of water
Meditate
Daily journaling
Exercise
Do something important
Do something good
Eat healthy
Read/listen to something good
Connect with others

WEEK OF:

MY PRIORITIES FOR THIS WEEK

GRATITUDE LOG:

MAIN GOALS:

DAILY ACTIVITIES

M T W T F S S

Daily gratitude log
Do something fun
8 glasses of water
Meditate
Daily journaling
Exercise
Do something important
Do something good
Eat healthy
Read/listen to something good
Connect with others

WEEK OF:

MY PRIORITIES FOR THIS WEEK

GRATITUDE LOG:

MAIN GOALS:

DAILY ACTIVITIES

	M	T	W	T	F	S	S
Daily gratitude log	○	○	○	○	○	○	○
Do something fun	○	○	○	○	○	○	○
8 glasses of water	○	○	○	○	○	○	○
Meditate	○	○	○	○	○	○	○
Daily journaling	○	○	○	○	○	○	○
Exercise	○	○	○	○	○	○	○
Do something important	○	○	○	○	○	○	○
Do something good	○	○	○	○	○	○	○
Eat healthy	○	○	○	○	○	○	○
Read/listen to something good	○	○	○	○	○	○	○
Connect with others	○	○	○	○	○	○	○

MY PRIORITIES FOR THIS WEEK

GRATITUDE LOG:

MAIN GOALS:

DAILY ACTIVITIES

	M	T	W	T	F	S	S
Daily gratitude log	○	○	○	○	○	○	○
Do something fun	○	○	○	○	○	○	○
8 glasses of water	○	○	○	○	○	○	○
Meditate	○	○	○	○	○	○	○
Daily journaling	○	○	○	○	○	○	○
Exercise	○	○	○	○	○	○	○
Do something important	○	○	○	○	○	○	○
Do something good	○	○	○	○	○	○	○
Eat healthy	○	○	○	○	○	○	○
Read/listen to something good	○	○	○	○	○	○	○
Connect with others	○	○	○	○	○	○	○

WEEK OF:

MY PRIORITIES FOR THIS WEEK

GRATITUDE LOG:

MAIN GOALS:

DAILY ACTIVITIES

	M	T	W	T	F	S	S
Daily gratitude log	○	○	○	○	○	○	○
Do something fun	○	○	○	○	○	○	○
8 glasses of water	○	○	○	○	○	○	○
Meditate	○	○	○	○	○	○	○
Daily journaling	○	○	○	○	○	○	○
Exercise	○	○	○	○	○	○	○
Do something important	○	○	○	○	○	○	○
Do something good	○	○	○	○	○	○	○
Eat healthy	○	○	○	○	○	○	○
Read/listen to something good	○	○	○	○	○	○	○
Connect with others	○	○	○	○	○	○	○

MY PRIORITIES FOR THIS WEEK

GRATITUDE LOG:

MAIN GOALS:

DAILY ACTIVITIES

	M	T	W	T	F	S	S
Daily gratitude log	◯	◯	◯	◯	◯	◯	◯
Do something fun	◯	◯	◯	◯	◯	◯	◯
8 glasses of water	◯	◯	◯	◯	◯	◯	◯
Meditate	◯	◯	◯	◯	◯	◯	◯
Daily journaling	◯	◯	◯	◯	◯	◯	◯
Exercise	◯	◯	◯	◯	◯	◯	◯
Do something important	◯	◯	◯	◯	◯	◯	◯
Do something good	◯	◯	◯	◯	◯	◯	◯
Eat healthy	◯	◯	◯	◯	◯	◯	◯
Read/listen to something good	◯	◯	◯	◯	◯	◯	◯
Connect with others	◯	◯	◯	◯	◯	◯	◯

WEEK OF:

MY PRIORITIES FOR THIS WEEK

GRATITUDE LOG:

MAIN GOALS:

DAILY ACTIVITIES

	M	T	W	T	F	S	S
Daily gratitude log	○	○	○	○	○	○	○
Do something fun	○	○	○	○	○	○	○
8 glasses of water	○	○	○	○	○	○	○
Meditate	○	○	○	○	○	○	○
Daily journaling	○	○	○	○	○	○	○
Exercise	○	○	○	○	○	○	○
Do something important	○	○	○	○	○	○	○
Do something good	○	○	○	○	○	○	○
Eat healthy	○	○	○	○	○	○	○
Read/listen to something good	○	○	○	○	○	○	○
Connect with others	○	○	○	○	○	○	○

MY PRIORITIES FOR THIS WEEK

GRATITUDE LOG:

MAIN GOALS:

DAILY ACTIVITIES

	M	T	W	T	F	S	S
Daily gratitude log	○	○	○	○	○	○	○
Do something fun	○	○	○	○	○	○	○
8 glasses of water	○	○	○	○	○	○	○
Meditate	○	○	○	○	○	○	○
Daily journaling	○	○	○	○	○	○	○
Exercise	○	○	○	○	○	○	○
Do something important	○	○	○	○	○	○	○
Do something good	○	○	○	○	○	○	○
Eat healthy	○	○	○	○	○	○	○
Read/listen to something good	○	○	○	○	○	○	○
Connect with others	○	○	○	○	○	○	○

WEEK OF:

MY PRIORITIES FOR THIS WEEK

GRATITUDE LOG:

MAIN GOALS:

DAILY ACTIVITIES

M T W T F S S

Daily gratitude log
Do something fun
8 glasses of water
Meditate
Daily journaling
Exercise
Do something important
Do something good
Eat healthy
Read/listen to something good
Connect with others

MY PRIORITIES FOR THIS WEEK

GRATITUDE LOG:

MAIN GOALS:

DAILY ACTIVITIES

	M	T	W	T	F	S	S
Daily gratitude log	○	○	○	○	○	○	○
Do something fun	○	○	○	○	○	○	○
8 glasses of water	○	○	○	○	○	○	○
Meditate	○	○	○	○	○	○	○
Daily journaling	○	○	○	○	○	○	○
Exercise	○	○	○	○	○	○	○
Do something important	○	○	○	○	○	○	○
Do something good	○	○	○	○	○	○	○
Eat healthy	○	○	○	○	○	○	○
Read/listen to something good	○	○	○	○	○	○	○
Connect with others	○	○	○	○	○	○	○

WEEK OF:

MY PRIORITIES FOR THIS WEEK

GRATITUDE LOG:

MAIN GOALS:

DAILY ACTIVITIES

	M	T	W	T	F	S	S
Daily gratitude log	○	○	○	○	○	○	○
Do something fun	○	○	○	○	○	○	○
8 glasses of water	○	○	○	○	○	○	○
Meditate	○	○	○	○	○	○	○
Daily journaling	○	○	○	○	○	○	○
Exercise	○	○	○	○	○	○	○
Do something important	○	○	○	○	○	○	○
Do something good	○	○	○	○	○	○	○
Eat healthy	○	○	○	○	○	○	○
Read/listen to something good	○	○	○	○	○	○	○
Connect with others	○	○	○	○	○	○	○

WEEK OF:

MY PRIORITIES FOR THIS WEEK

GRATITUDE LOG:

MAIN GOALS:

DAILY ACTIVITIES

M T W T F S S

Daily gratitude log
Do something fun
8 glasses of water
Meditate
Daily journaling
Exercise
Do something important
Do something good
Eat healthy
Read/listen to something good
Connect with others

WEEK OF:

MY PRIORITIES FOR THIS WEEK

GRATITUDE LOG:

MAIN GOALS:

DAILY ACTIVITIES

	M	T	W	T	F	S	S
Daily gratitude log	○	○	○	○	○	○	○
Do something fun	○	○	○	○	○	○	○
8 glasses of water	○	○	○	○	○	○	○
Meditate	○	○	○	○	○	○	○
Daily journaling	○	○	○	○	○	○	○
Exercise	○	○	○	○	○	○	○
Do something important	○	○	○	○	○	○	○
Do something good	○	○	○	○	○	○	○
Eat healthy	○	○	○	○	○	○	○
Read/listen to something good	○	○	○	○	○	○	○
Connect with others	○	○	○	○	○	○	○

WEEK OF:

MY PRIORITIES FOR THIS WEEK

GRATITUDE LOG:

MAIN GOALS:

DAILY ACTIVITIES

	M	T	W	T	F	S	S
Daily gratitude log	○	○	○	○	○	○	○
Do something fun	○	○	○	○	○	○	○
8 glasses of water	○	○	○	○	○	○	○
Meditate	○	○	○	○	○	○	○
Daily journaling	○	○	○	○	○	○	○
Exercise	○	○	○	○	○	○	○
Do something important	○	○	○	○	○	○	○
Do something good	○	○	○	○	○	○	○
Eat healthy	○	○	○	○	○	○	○
Read/listen to something good	○	○	○	○	○	○	○
Connect with others	○	○	○	○	○	○	○

MY PRIORITIES FOR THIS WEEK

GRATITUDE LOG:

MAIN GOALS:

DAILY ACTIVITIES

	M	T	W	T	F	S	S
Daily gratitude log	○	○	○	○	○	○	○
Do something fun	○	○	○	○	○	○	○
8 glasses of water	○	○	○	○	○	○	○
Meditate	○	○	○	○	○	○	○
Daily journaling	○	○	○	○	○	○	○
Exercise	○	○	○	○	○	○	○
Do something important	○	○	○	○	○	○	○
Do something good	○	○	○	○	○	○	○
Eat healthy	○	○	○	○	○	○	○
Read/listen to something good	○	○	○	○	○	○	○
Connect with others	○	○	○	○	○	○	○

WEEK OF:

MY PRIORITIES FOR THIS WEEK

GRATITUDE LOG:

MAIN GOALS:

DAILY ACTIVITIES

	M	T	W	T	F	S	S
Daily gratitude log	○	○	○	○	○	○	○
Do something fun	○	○	○	○	○	○	○
8 glasses of water	○	○	○	○	○	○	○
Meditate	○	○	○	○	○	○	○
Daily journaling	○	○	○	○	○	○	○
Exercise	○	○	○	○	○	○	○
Do something important	○	○	○	○	○	○	○
Do something good	○	○	○	○	○	○	○
Eat healthy	○	○	○	○	○	○	○
Read/listen to something good	○	○	○	○	○	○	○
Connect with others	○	○	○	○	○	○	○

WEEK OF:

MY PRIORITIES FOR THIS WEEK

GRATITUDE LOG:

MAIN GOALS:

DAILY ACTIVITIES

	M	T	W	T	F	S	S
Daily gratitude log	○	○	○	○	○	○	○
Do something fun	○	○	○	○	○	○	○
8 glasses of water	○	○	○	○	○	○	○
Meditate	○	○	○	○	○	○	○
Daily journaling	○	○	○	○	○	○	○
Exercise	○	○	○	○	○	○	○
Do something important	○	○	○	○	○	○	○
Do something good	○	○	○	○	○	○	○
Eat healthy	○	○	○	○	○	○	○
Read/listen to something good	○	○	○	○	○	○	○
Connect with others	○	○	○	○	○	○	○

live
your
dream.

WEEK OF:

MY PRIORITIES FOR THIS WEEK

GRATITUDE LOG:

MAIN GOALS:

DAILY ACTIVITIES

	M	T	W	T	F	S	S
Daily gratitude log	○	○	○	○	○	○	○
Do something fun	○	○	○	○	○	○	○
8 glasses of water	○	○	○	○	○	○	○
Meditate	○	○	○	○	○	○	○
Daily journaling	○	○	○	○	○	○	○
Exercise	○	○	○	○	○	○	○
Do something important	○	○	○	○	○	○	○
Do something good	○	○	○	○	○	○	○
Eat healthy	○	○	○	○	○	○	○
Read/listen to something good	○	○	○	○	○	○	○
Connect with others	○	○	○	○	○	○	○

WEEK OF:

MY PRIORITIES FOR THIS WEEK

GRATITUDE LOG:

MAIN GOALS:

DAILY ACTIVITIES

M T W T F S S

Daily gratitude log
Do something fun
8 glasses of water
Meditate
Daily journaling
Exercise
Do something important
Do something good
Eat healthy
Read/listen to something good
Connect with others

WEEK OF:

MY PRIORITIES FOR THIS WEEK

GRATITUDE LOG:

MAIN GOALS:

DAILY ACTIVITIES

	M	T	W	T	F	S	S
Daily gratitude log	○	○	○	○	○	○	○
Do something fun	○	○	○	○	○	○	○
8 glasses of water	○	○	○	○	○	○	○
Meditate	○	○	○	○	○	○	○
Daily journaling	○	○	○	○	○	○	○
Exercise	○	○	○	○	○	○	○
Do something important	○	○	○	○	○	○	○
Do something good	○	○	○	○	○	○	○
Eat healthy	○	○	○	○	○	○	○
Read/listen to something good	○	○	○	○	○	○	○
Connect with others	○	○	○	○	○	○	○

WEEK OF:

MY PRIORITIES FOR THIS WEEK

GRATITUDE LOG:

MAIN GOALS:

DAILY ACTIVITIES

M T W T F S S

Daily gratitude log
Do something fun
8 glasses of water
Meditate
Daily journaling
Exercise
Do something important
Do something good
Eat healthy
Read/listen to something good
Connect with others

WEEK OF:

MY PRIORITIES FOR THIS WEEK

GRATITUDE LOG:

MAIN GOALS:

DAILY ACTIVITIES

	M	T	W	T	F	S	S
Daily gratitude log	○	○	○	○	○	○	○
Do something fun	○	○	○	○	○	○	○
8 glasses of water	○	○	○	○	○	○	○
Meditate	○	○	○	○	○	○	○
Daily journaling	○	○	○	○	○	○	○
Exercise	○	○	○	○	○	○	○
Do something important	○	○	○	○	○	○	○
Do something good	○	○	○	○	○	○	○
Eat healthy	○	○	○	○	○	○	○
Read/listen to something good	○	○	○	○	○	○	○
Connect with others	○	○	○	○	○	○	○

WEEK OF:

MY PRIORITIES FOR THIS WEEK

GRATITUDE LOG:

MAIN GOALS:

DAILY ACTIVITIES

M T W T F S S

Daily gratitude log
Do something fun
8 glasses of water
Meditate
Daily journaling
Exercise
Do something important
Do something good
Eat healthy
Read/listen to something good
Connect with others

WEEK OF:

MY PRIORITIES FOR THIS WEEK

GRATITUDE LOG:

MAIN GOALS:

DAILY ACTIVITIES

	M	T	W	T	F	S	S
Daily gratitude log	○	○	○	○	○	○	○
Do something fun	○	○	○	○	○	○	○
8 glasses of water	○	○	○	○	○	○	○
Meditate	○	○	○	○	○	○	○
Daily journaling	○	○	○	○	○	○	○
Exercise	○	○	○	○	○	○	○
Do something important	○	○	○	○	○	○	○
Do something good	○	○	○	○	○	○	○
Eat healthy	○	○	○	○	○	○	○
Read/listen to something good	○	○	○	○	○	○	○
Connect with others	○	○	○	○	○	○	○

WEEK OF:

MY PRIORITIES FOR THIS WEEK

GRATITUDE LOG:

MAIN GOALS:

DAILY ACTIVITIES

	M	T	W	T	F	S	S
Daily gratitude log	○	○	○	○	○	○	○
Do something fun	○	○	○	○	○	○	○
8 glasses of water	○	○	○	○	○	○	○
Meditate	○	○	○	○	○	○	○
Daily journaling	○	○	○	○	○	○	○
Exercise	○	○	○	○	○	○	○
Do something important	○	○	○	○	○	○	○
Do something good	○	○	○	○	○	○	○
Eat healthy	○	○	○	○	○	○	○
Read/listen to something good	○	○	○	○	○	○	○
Connect with others	○	○	○	○	○	○	○

WEEK OF:

MY PRIORITIES FOR THIS WEEK

GRATITUDE LOG:

MAIN GOALS:

DAILY ACTIVITIES

	M	T	W	T	F	S	S
Daily gratitude log	○	○	○	○	○	○	○
Do something fun	○	○	○	○	○	○	○
8 glasses of water	○	○	○	○	○	○	○
Meditate	○	○	○	○	○	○	○
Daily journaling	○	○	○	○	○	○	○
Exercise	○	○	○	○	○	○	○
Do something important	○	○	○	○	○	○	○
Do something good	○	○	○	○	○	○	○
Eat healthy	○	○	○	○	○	○	○
Read/listen to something good	○	○	○	○	○	○	○
Connect with others	○	○	○	○	○	○	○

WEEK OF:

MY PRIORITIES FOR THIS WEEK

GRATITUDE LOG:

MAIN GOALS:

DAILY ACTIVITIES

	M	T	W	T	F	S	S
Daily gratitude log	○	○	○	○	○	○	○
Do something fun	○	○	○	○	○	○	○
8 glasses of water	○	○	○	○	○	○	○
Meditate	○	○	○	○	○	○	○
Daily journaling	○	○	○	○	○	○	○
Exercise	○	○	○	○	○	○	○
Do something important	○	○	○	○	○	○	○
Do something good	○	○	○	○	○	○	○
Eat healthy	○	○	○	○	○	○	○
Read/listen to something good	○	○	○	○	○	○	○
Connect with others	○	○	○	○	○	○	○

WEEK OF:

MY PRIORITIES FOR THIS WEEK

GRATITUDE LOG:

MAIN GOALS:

DAILY ACTIVITIES

	M	T	W	T	F	S	S
Daily gratitude log	○	○	○	○	○	○	○
Do something fun	○	○	○	○	○	○	○
8 glasses of water	○	○	○	○	○	○	○
Meditate	○	○	○	○	○	○	○
Daily journaling	○	○	○	○	○	○	○
Exercise	○	○	○	○	○	○	○
Do something important	○	○	○	○	○	○	○
Do something good	○	○	○	○	○	○	○
Eat healthy	○	○	○	○	○	○	○
Read/listen to something good	○	○	○	○	○	○	○
Connect with others	○	○	○	○	○	○	○

WEEK OF:

MY PRIORITIES FOR THIS WEEK

GRATITUDE LOG:

MAIN GOALS:

DAILY ACTIVITIES

	M	T	W	T	F	S	S
Daily gratitude log	○	○	○	○	○	○	○
Do something fun	○	○	○	○	○	○	○
8 glasses of water	○	○	○	○	○	○	○
Meditate	○	○	○	○	○	○	○
Daily journaling	○	○	○	○	○	○	○
Exercise	○	○	○	○	○	○	○
Do something important	○	○	○	○	○	○	○
Do something good	○	○	○	○	○	○	○
Eat healthy	○	○	○	○	○	○	○
Read/listen to something good	○	○	○	○	○	○	○
Connect with others	○	○	○	○	○	○	○

WEEK OF:

MY PRIORITIES FOR THIS WEEK

GRATITUDE LOG:

MAIN GOALS:

DAILY ACTIVITIES

	M	T	W	T	F	S	S
Daily gratitude log	○	○	○	○	○	○	○
Do something fun	○	○	○	○	○	○	○
8 glasses of water	○	○	○	○	○	○	○
Meditate	○	○	○	○	○	○	○
Daily journaling	○	○	○	○	○	○	○
Exercise	○	○	○	○	○	○	○
Do something important	○	○	○	○	○	○	○
Do something good	○	○	○	○	○	○	○
Eat healthy	○	○	○	○	○	○	○
Read/listen to something good	○	○	○	○	○	○	○
Connect with others	○	○	○	○	○	○	○

WEEK OF:

MY PRIORITIES FOR THIS WEEK

GRATITUDE LOG:

MAIN GOALS:

DAILY ACTIVITIES

M T W T F S S

Daily gratitude log
Do something fun
8 glasses of water
Meditate
Daily journaling
Exercise
Do something important
Do something good
Eat healthy
Read/listen to something good
Connect with others

WEEK OF:

MY PRIORITIES FOR THIS WEEK

GRATITUDE LOG:

MAIN GOALS:

DAILY ACTIVITIES

	M	T	W	T	F	S	S
Daily gratitude log	○	○	○	○	○	○	○
Do something fun	○	○	○	○	○	○	○
8 glasses of water	○	○	○	○	○	○	○
Meditate	○	○	○	○	○	○	○
Daily journaling	○	○	○	○	○	○	○
Exercise	○	○	○	○	○	○	○
Do something important	○	○	○	○	○	○	○
Do something good	○	○	○	○	○	○	○
Eat healthy	○	○	○	○	○	○	○
Read/listen to something good	○	○	○	○	○	○	○
Connect with others	○	○	○	○	○	○	○

WEEK OF:

MY PRIORITIES FOR THIS WEEK

GRATITUDE LOG:

MAIN GOALS:

DAILY ACTIVITIES

	M	T	W	T	F	S	S
Daily gratitude log	○	○	○	○	○	○	○
Do something fun	○	○	○	○	○	○	○
8 glasses of water	○	○	○	○	○	○	○
Meditate	○	○	○	○	○	○	○
Daily journaling	○	○	○	○	○	○	○
Exercise	○	○	○	○	○	○	○
Do something important	○	○	○	○	○	○	○
Do something good	○	○	○	○	○	○	○
Eat healthy	○	○	○	○	○	○	○
Read/listen to something good	○	○	○	○	○	○	○
Connect with others	○	○	○	○	○	○	○

WEEK OF:

MY PRIORITIES FOR THIS WEEK

GRATITUDE LOG:

MAIN GOALS:

DAILY ACTIVITIES

M T W T F S S

Daily gratitude log
Do something fun
8 glasses of water
Meditate
Daily journaling
Exercise
Do something
important
Do something good
Eat healthy
Read/listen
to something good
Connect with others

WEEK OF:

MY PRIORITIES FOR THIS WEEK

GRATITUDE LOG:

MAIN GOALS:

DAILY ACTIVITIES

M T W T F S S

Daily gratitude log
Do something fun
8 glasses of water
Meditate
Daily journaling
Exercise
Do something important
Do something good
Eat healthy
Read/listen to something good
Connect with others

WEEK OF:

MY PRIORITIES FOR THIS WEEK

GRATITUDE LOG:

MAIN GOALS:

DAILY ACTIVITIES

	M	T	W	T	F	S	S
Daily gratitude log	○	○	○	○	○	○	○
Do something fun	○	○	○	○	○	○	○
8 glasses of water	○	○	○	○	○	○	○
Meditate	○	○	○	○	○	○	○
Daily journaling	○	○	○	○	○	○	○
Exercise	○	○	○	○	○	○	○
Do something important	○	○	○	○	○	○	○
Do something good	○	○	○	○	○	○	○
Eat healthy	○	○	○	○	○	○	○
Read/listen to something good	○	○	○	○	○	○	○
Connect with others	○	○	○	○	○	○	○

WEEK OF:

MY PRIORITIES FOR THIS WEEK

GRATITUDE LOG:

MAIN GOALS:

DAILY ACTIVITIES

	M	T	W	T	F	S	S
Daily gratitude log	◯	◯	◯	◯	◯	◯	◯
Do something fun	◯	◯	◯	◯	◯	◯	◯
8 glasses of water	◯	◯	◯	◯	◯	◯	◯
Meditate	◯	◯	◯	◯	◯	◯	◯
Daily journaling	◯	◯	◯	◯	◯	◯	◯
Exercise	◯	◯	◯	◯	◯	◯	◯
Do something important	◯	◯	◯	◯	◯	◯	◯
Do something good	◯	◯	◯	◯	◯	◯	◯
Eat healthy	◯	◯	◯	◯	◯	◯	◯
Read/listen to something good	◯	◯	◯	◯	◯	◯	◯
Connect with others	◯	◯	◯	◯	◯	◯	◯

WEEK OF:

MY PRIORITIES FOR THIS WEEK

GRATITUDE LOG:

MAIN GOALS:

DAILY ACTIVITIES

	M	T	W	T	F	S	S
Daily gratitude log	○	○	○	○	○	○	○
Do something fun	○	○	○	○	○	○	○
8 glasses of water	○	○	○	○	○	○	○
Meditate	○	○	○	○	○	○	○
Daily journaling	○	○	○	○	○	○	○
Exercise	○	○	○	○	○	○	○
Do something important	○	○	○	○	○	○	○
Do something good	○	○	○	○	○	○	○
Eat healthy	○	○	○	○	○	○	○
Read/listen to something good	○	○	○	○	○	○	○
Connect with others	○	○	○	○	○	○	○

WEEK OF:

MY PRIORITIES FOR THIS WEEK

GRATITUDE LOG:

MAIN GOALS:

DAILY ACTIVITIES

	M	T	W	T	F	S	S
Daily gratitude log	○	○	○	○	○	○	○
Do something fun	○	○	○	○	○	○	○
8 glasses of water	○	○	○	○	○	○	○
Meditate	○	○	○	○	○	○	○
Daily journaling	○	○	○	○	○	○	○
Exercise	○	○	○	○	○	○	○
Do something important	○	○	○	○	○	○	○
Do something good	○	○	○	○	○	○	○
Eat healthy	○	○	○	○	○	○	○
Read/listen to something good	○	○	○	○	○	○	○
Connect with others	○	○	○	○	○	○	○

WEEK OF:

MY PRIORITIES FOR THIS WEEK

GRATITUDE LOG:

MAIN GOALS:

DAILY ACTIVITIES

	M	T	W	T	F	S	S
Daily gratitude log	○	○	○	○	○	○	○
Do something fun	○	○	○	○	○	○	○
8 glasses of water	○	○	○	○	○	○	○
Meditate	○	○	○	○	○	○	○
Daily journaling	○	○	○	○	○	○	○
Exercise	○	○	○	○	○	○	○
Do something important	○	○	○	○	○	○	○
Do something good	○	○	○	○	○	○	○
Eat healthy	○	○	○	○	○	○	○
Read/listen to something good	○	○	○	○	○	○	○
Connect with others	○	○	○	○	○	○	○

MY PRIORITIES FOR THIS WEEK

GRATITUDE LOG:

MAIN GOALS:

DAILY ACTIVITIES

	M	T	W	T	F	S	S
Daily gratitude log	○	○	○	○	○	○	○
Do something fun	○	○	○	○	○	○	○
8 glasses of water	○	○	○	○	○	○	○
Meditate	○	○	○	○	○	○	○
Daily journaling	○	○	○	○	○	○	○
Exercise	○	○	○	○	○	○	○
Do something important	○	○	○	○	○	○	○
Do something good	○	○	○	○	○	○	○
Eat healthy	○	○	○	○	○	○	○
Read/listen to something good	○	○	○	○	○	○	○
Connect with others	○	○	○	○	○	○	○

WEEK OF:

MY PRIORITIES FOR THIS WEEK

GRATITUDE LOG:

MAIN GOALS:

DAILY ACTIVITIES

M T W T F S S

Daily gratitude log
Do something fun
8 glasses of water
Meditate
Daily journaling
Exercise
Do something important
Do something good
Eat healthy
Read/listen to something good
Connect with others

WEEK OF:

MY PRIORITIES FOR THIS WEEK

GRATITUDE LOG:

MAIN GOALS:

DAILY ACTIVITIES

	M	T	W	T	F	S	S
Daily gratitude log	○	○	○	○	○	○	○
Do something fun	○	○	○	○	○	○	○
8 glasses of water	○	○	○	○	○	○	○
Meditate	○	○	○	○	○	○	○
Daily journaling	○	○	○	○	○	○	○
Exercise	○	○	○	○	○	○	○
Do something important	○	○	○	○	○	○	○
Do something good	○	○	○	○	○	○	○
Eat healthy	○	○	○	○	○	○	○
Read/listen to something good	○	○	○	○	○	○	○
Connect with others	○	○	○	○	○	○	○

WEEK OF:

MY PRIORITIES FOR THIS WEEK

GRATITUDE LOG:

MAIN GOALS:

DAILY ACTIVITIES

	M	T	W	T	F	S	S
Daily gratitude log	○	○	○	○	○	○	○
Do something fun	○	○	○	○	○	○	○
8 glasses of water	○	○	○	○	○	○	○
Meditate	○	○	○	○	○	○	○
Daily journaling	○	○	○	○	○	○	○
Exercise	○	○	○	○	○	○	○
Do something important	○	○	○	○	○	○	○
Do something good	○	○	○	○	○	○	○
Eat healthy	○	○	○	○	○	○	○
Read/listen to something good	○	○	○	○	○	○	○
Connect with others	○	○	○	○	○	○	○

MY PRIORITIES FOR THIS WEEK

GRATITUDE LOG:

MAIN GOALS:

DAILY ACTIVITIES

	M	T	W	T	F	S	S
Daily gratitude log	○	○	○	○	○	○	○
Do something fun	○	○	○	○	○	○	○
8 glasses of water	○	○	○	○	○	○	○
Meditate	○	○	○	○	○	○	○
Daily journaling	○	○	○	○	○	○	○
Exercise	○	○	○	○	○	○	○
Do something important	○	○	○	○	○	○	○
Do something good	○	○	○	○	○	○	○
Eat healthy	○	○	○	○	○	○	○
Read/listen to something good	○	○	○	○	○	○	○
Connect with others	○	○	○	○	○	○	○

WEEK OF:

MY PRIORITIES FOR THIS WEEK

GRATITUDE LOG:

MAIN GOALS:

DAILY ACTIVITIES

	M	T	W	T	F	S	S
Daily gratitude log	○	○	○	○	○	○	○
Do something fun	○	○	○	○	○	○	○
8 glasses of water	○	○	○	○	○	○	○
Meditate	○	○	○	○	○	○	○
Daily journaling	○	○	○	○	○	○	○
Exercise	○	○	○	○	○	○	○
Do something important	○	○	○	○	○	○	○
Do something good	○	○	○	○	○	○	○
Eat healthy	○	○	○	○	○	○	○
Read/listen to something good	○	○	○	○	○	○	○
Connect with others	○	○	○	○	○	○	○

WEEK OF:

MY PRIORITIES FOR THIS WEEK

GRATITUDE LOG:

MAIN GOALS:

DAILY ACTIVITIES

	M	T	W	T	F	S	S
Daily gratitude log	○	○	○	○	○	○	○
Do something fun	○	○	○	○	○	○	○
8 glasses of water	○	○	○	○	○	○	○
Meditate	○	○	○	○	○	○	○
Daily journaling	○	○	○	○	○	○	○
Exercise	○	○	○	○	○	○	○
Do something important	○	○	○	○	○	○	○
Do something good	○	○	○	○	○	○	○
Eat healthy	○	○	○	○	○	○	○
Read/listen to something good	○	○	○	○	○	○	○
Connect with others	○	○	○	○	○	○	○

WEEK OF:

MY PRIORITIES FOR THIS WEEK

GRATITUDE LOG:

MAIN GOALS:

DAILY ACTIVITIES

	M	T	W	T	F	S	S
Daily gratitude log	○	○	○	○	○	○	○
Do something fun	○	○	○	○	○	○	○
8 glasses of water	○	○	○	○	○	○	○
Meditate	○	○	○	○	○	○	○
Daily journaling	○	○	○	○	○	○	○
Exercise	○	○	○	○	○	○	○
Do something important	○	○	○	○	○	○	○
Do something good	○	○	○	○	○	○	○
Eat healthy	○	○	○	○	○	○	○
Read/listen to something good	○	○	○	○	○	○	○
Connect with others	○	○	○	○	○	○	○

WEEK OF:

MY PRIORITIES FOR THIS WEEK

GRATITUDE LOG:

MAIN GOALS:

DAILY ACTIVITIES

	M	T	W	T	F	S	S
Daily gratitude log	○	○	○	○	○	○	○
Do something fun	○	○	○	○	○	○	○
8 glasses of water	○	○	○	○	○	○	○
Meditate	○	○	○	○	○	○	○
Daily journaling	○	○	○	○	○	○	○
Exercise	○	○	○	○	○	○	○
Do something important	○	○	○	○	○	○	○
Do something good	○	○	○	○	○	○	○
Eat healthy	○	○	○	○	○	○	○
Read/listen to something good	○	○	○	○	○	○	○
Connect with others	○	○	○	○	○	○	○

WEEK OF:

MY PRIORITIES FOR THIS WEEK

GRATITUDE LOG:

MAIN GOALS:

DAILY ACTIVITIES

M T W T F S S

Daily gratitude log
Do something fun
8 glasses of water
Meditate
Daily journaling
Exercise
Do something important
Do something good
Eat healthy
Read/listen to something good
Connect with others

WEEK OF:

MY PRIORITIES FOR THIS WEEK

GRATITUDE LOG:

MAIN GOALS:

DAILY ACTIVITIES

M T W T F S S

Daily gratitude log
Do something fun
8 glasses of water
Meditate
Daily journaling
Exercise
Do something
important
Do something good
Eat healthy
Read/listen
to something good
Connect with others

WEEK OF:

MY PRIORITIES FOR THIS WEEK

GRATITUDE LOG:

MAIN GOALS:

DAILY ACTIVITIES

	M	T	W	T	F	S	S
Daily gratitude log	○	○	○	○	○	○	○
Do something fun	○	○	○	○	○	○	○
8 glasses of water	○	○	○	○	○	○	○
Meditate	○	○	○	○	○	○	○
Daily journaling	○	○	○	○	○	○	○
Exercise	○	○	○	○	○	○	○
Do something important	○	○	○	○	○	○	○
Do something good	○	○	○	○	○	○	○
Eat healthy	○	○	○	○	○	○	○
Read/listen to something good	○	○	○	○	○	○	○
Connect with others	○	○	○	○	○	○	○

WEEK OF:

MY PRIORITIES FOR THIS WEEK

GRATITUDE LOG:

MAIN GOALS:

DAILY ACTIVITIES

	M	T	W	T	F	S	S
Daily gratitude log	○	○	○	○	○	○	○
Do something fun	○	○	○	○	○	○	○
8 glasses of water	○	○	○	○	○	○	○
Meditate	○	○	○	○	○	○	○
Daily journaling	○	○	○	○	○	○	○
Exercise	○	○	○	○	○	○	○
Do something important	○	○	○	○	○	○	○
Do something good	○	○	○	○	○	○	○
Eat healthy	○	○	○	○	○	○	○
Read/listen to something good	○	○	○	○	○	○	○
Connect with others	○	○	○	○	○	○	○

WEEK OF:

MY PRIORITIES FOR THIS WEEK

GRATITUDE LOG:

MAIN GOALS:

DAILY ACTIVITIES

	M	T	W	T	F	S	S
Daily gratitude log	○	○	○	○	○	○	○
Do something fun	○	○	○	○	○	○	○
8 glasses of water	○	○	○	○	○	○	○
Meditate	○	○	○	○	○	○	○
Daily journaling	○	○	○	○	○	○	○
Exercise	○	○	○	○	○	○	○
Do something important	○	○	○	○	○	○	○
Do something good	○	○	○	○	○	○	○
Eat healthy	○	○	○	○	○	○	○
Read/listen to something good	○	○	○	○	○	○	○
Connect with others	○	○	○	○	○	○	○

WEEK OF:

MY PRIORITIES FOR THIS WEEK

GRATITUDE LOG:

MAIN GOALS:

DAILY ACTIVITIES

M T W T F S S

Daily gratitude log
Do something fun
8 glasses of water
Meditate
Daily journaling
Exercise
Do something important
Do something good
Eat healthy
Read/listen to something good
Connect with others

WEEK OF:

MY PRIORITIES FOR THIS WEEK

GRATITUDE LOG:

MAIN GOALS:

DAILY ACTIVITIES

	M	T	W	T	F	S	S
Daily gratitude log	○	○	○	○	○	○	○
Do something fun	○	○	○	○	○	○	○
8 glasses of water	○	○	○	○	○	○	○
Meditate	○	○	○	○	○	○	○
Daily journaling	○	○	○	○	○	○	○
Exercise	○	○	○	○	○	○	○
Do something important	○	○	○	○	○	○	○
Do something good	○	○	○	○	○	○	○
Eat healthy	○	○	○	○	○	○	○
Read/listen to something good	○	○	○	○	○	○	○
Connect with others	○	○	○	○	○	○	○

WEEK OF:

MY PRIORITIES FOR THIS WEEK

GRATITUDE LOG:

MAIN GOALS:

DAILY ACTIVITIES

M T W T F S S

Daily gratitude log
Do something fun
8 glasses of water
Meditate
Daily journaling
Exercise
Do something important
Do something good
Eat healthy
Read/listen to something good
Connect with others

WEEK OF:

MY PRIORITIES FOR THIS WEEK

GRATITUDE LOG:

MAIN GOALS:

DAILY ACTIVITIES

M T W T F S S

Daily gratitude log
Do something fun
8 glasses of water
Meditate
Daily journaling
Exercise
Do something important
Do something good
Eat healthy
Read/listen to something good
Connect with others

WEEK OF:

MY PRIORITIES FOR THIS WEEK

GRATITUDE LOG:

MAIN GOALS:

DAILY ACTIVITIES

	M	T	W	T	F	S	S
Daily gratitude log	○	○	○	○	○	○	○
Do something fun	○	○	○	○	○	○	○
8 glasses of water	○	○	○	○	○	○	○
Meditate	○	○	○	○	○	○	○
Daily journaling	○	○	○	○	○	○	○
Exercise	○	○	○	○	○	○	○
Do something important	○	○	○	○	○	○	○
Do something good	○	○	○	○	○	○	○
Eat healthy	○	○	○	○	○	○	○
Read/listen to something good	○	○	○	○	○	○	○
Connect with others	○	○	○	○	○	○	○

MY PRIORITIES FOR THIS WEEK

GRATITUDE LOG:

MAIN GOALS:

DAILY ACTIVITIES

	M	T	W	T	F	S	S
Daily gratitude log	○	○	○	○	○	○	○
Do something fun	○	○	○	○	○	○	○
8 glasses of water	○	○	○	○	○	○	○
Meditate	○	○	○	○	○	○	○
Daily journaling	○	○	○	○	○	○	○
Exercise	○	○	○	○	○	○	○
Do something important	○	○	○	○	○	○	○
Do something good	○	○	○	○	○	○	○
Eat healthy	○	○	○	○	○	○	○
Read/listen to something good	○	○	○	○	○	○	○
Connect with others	○	○	○	○	○	○	○

WEEK OF:

MY PRIORITIES FOR THIS WEEK

GRATITUDE LOG:

MAIN GOALS:

DAILY ACTIVITIES

	M	T	W	T	F	S	S
Daily gratitude log	○	○	○	○	○	○	○
Do something fun	○	○	○	○	○	○	○
8 glasses of water	○	○	○	○	○	○	○
Meditate	○	○	○	○	○	○	○
Daily journaling	○	○	○	○	○	○	○
Exercise	○	○	○	○	○	○	○
Do something important	○	○	○	○	○	○	○
Do something good	○	○	○	○	○	○	○
Eat healthy	○	○	○	○	○	○	○
Read/listen to something good	○	○	○	○	○	○	○
Connect with others	○	○	○	○	○	○	○

WEEK OF:

MY PRIORITIES FOR THIS WEEK

GRATITUDE LOG:

MAIN GOALS:

DAILY ACTIVITIES

	M	T	W	T	F	S	S
Daily gratitude log	○	○	○	○	○	○	○
Do something fun	○	○	○	○	○	○	○
8 glasses of water	○	○	○	○	○	○	○
Meditate	○	○	○	○	○	○	○
Daily journaling	○	○	○	○	○	○	○
Exercise	○	○	○	○	○	○	○
Do something important	○	○	○	○	○	○	○
Do something good	○	○	○	○	○	○	○
Eat healthy	○	○	○	○	○	○	○
Read/listen to something good	○	○	○	○	○	○	○
Connect with others	○	○	○	○	○	○	○

WEEK OF:

MY PRIORITIES FOR THIS WEEK

GRATITUDE LOG:

MAIN GOALS:

DAILY ACTIVITIES

	M	T	W	T	F	S	S
Daily gratitude log	○	○	○	○	○	○	○
Do something fun	○	○	○	○	○	○	○
8 glasses of water	○	○	○	○	○	○	○
Meditate	○	○	○	○	○	○	○
Daily journaling	○	○	○	○	○	○	○
Exercise	○	○	○	○	○	○	○
Do something important	○	○	○	○	○	○	○
Do something good	○	○	○	○	○	○	○
Eat healthy	○	○	○	○	○	○	○
Read/listen to something good	○	○	○	○	○	○	○
Connect with others	○	○	○	○	○	○	○

WEEK OF:

MY PRIORITIES FOR THIS WEEK

GRATITUDE LOG:

MAIN GOALS:

DAILY ACTIVITIES

	M	T	W	T	F	S	S
Daily gratitude log	○	○	○	○	○	○	○
Do something fun	○	○	○	○	○	○	○
8 glasses of water	○	○	○	○	○	○	○
Meditate	○	○	○	○	○	○	○
Daily journaling	○	○	○	○	○	○	○
Exercise	○	○	○	○	○	○	○
Do something important	○	○	○	○	○	○	○
Do something good	○	○	○	○	○	○	○
Eat healthy	○	○	○	○	○	○	○
Read/listen to something good	○	○	○	○	○	○	○
Connect with others	○	○	○	○	○	○	○

MY PRIORITIES FOR THIS WEEK

GRATITUDE LOG:

MAIN GOALS:

DAILY ACTIVITIES

	M	T	W	T	F	S	S
Daily gratitude log	○	○	○	○	○	○	○
Do something fun	○	○	○	○	○	○	○
8 glasses of water	○	○	○	○	○	○	○
Meditate	○	○	○	○	○	○	○
Daily journaling	○	○	○	○	○	○	○
Exercise	○	○	○	○	○	○	○
Do something important	○	○	○	○	○	○	○
Do something good	○	○	○	○	○	○	○
Eat healthy	○	○	○	○	○	○	○
Read/listen to something good	○	○	○	○	○	○	○
Connect with others	○	○	○	○	○	○	○

WEEK OF:

MY PRIORITIES FOR THIS WEEK

GRATITUDE LOG:

MAIN GOALS:

DAILY ACTIVITIES

M T W T F S S

Daily gratitude log
Do something fun
8 glasses of water
Meditate
Daily journaling
Exercise
Do something important
Do something good
Eat healthy
Read/listen to something good
Connect with others

WEEK OF:

MY PRIORITIES FOR THIS WEEK

GRATITUDE LOG:

MAIN GOALS:

DAILY ACTIVITIES

	M	T	W	T	F	S	S
Daily gratitude log	○	○	○	○	○	○	○
Do something fun	○	○	○	○	○	○	○
8 glasses of water	○	○	○	○	○	○	○
Meditate	○	○	○	○	○	○	○
Daily journaling	○	○	○	○	○	○	○
Exercise	○	○	○	○	○	○	○
Do something important	○	○	○	○	○	○	○
Do something good	○	○	○	○	○	○	○
Eat healthy	○	○	○	○	○	○	○
Read/listen to something good	○	○	○	○	○	○	○
Connect with others	○	○	○	○	○	○	○

WEEK OF:

MY PRIORITIES FOR THIS WEEK

GRATITUDE LOG:

MAIN GOALS:

DAILY ACTIVITIES

	M	T	W	T	F	S	S
Daily gratitude log	○	○	○	○	○	○	○
Do something fun	○	○	○	○	○	○	○
8 glasses of water	○	○	○	○	○	○	○
Meditate	○	○	○	○	○	○	○
Daily journaling	○	○	○	○	○	○	○
Exercise	○	○	○	○	○	○	○
Do something important	○	○	○	○	○	○	○
Do something good	○	○	○	○	○	○	○
Eat healthy	○	○	○	○	○	○	○
Read/listen to something good	○	○	○	○	○	○	○
Connect with others	○	○	○	○	○	○	○

MY PRIORITIES FOR THIS WEEK

GRATITUDE LOG:

MAIN GOALS:

DAILY ACTIVITIES

	M	T	W	T	F	S	S
Daily gratitude log	○	○	○	○	○	○	○
Do something fun	○	○	○	○	○	○	○
8 glasses of water	○	○	○	○	○	○	○
Meditate	○	○	○	○	○	○	○
Daily journaling	○	○	○	○	○	○	○
Exercise	○	○	○	○	○	○	○
Do something important	○	○	○	○	○	○	○
Do something good	○	○	○	○	○	○	○
Eat healthy	○	○	○	○	○	○	○
Read/listen to something good	○	○	○	○	○	○	○
Connect with others	○	○	○	○	○	○	○

live
your
dream.